What Horses Say

KENILWORTH PRESS

What Horses Say

HOW TO HEAR, HELP AND HEAL THEM

Anna Clemence Mews & Julie Dicker

Foreword by Joanna Lumley

First published in Great Britain in 2004 by
Kenilworth Press
An imprint of Quiller Publishing Ltd
Wykey House, Wykey, Shrewsbury, SY4 1JA
Tel: 01939 261616 Fax: 01939 261606
E-mail: info@quillerbooks.com
Website: www.kenilworthpress.co.uk

Reprinted in 2005 and 2007

Published simultaneously in the United States of America by
Trafalgar Square Publishing, North Pomfret, Vermont 05053

Disclaimer of Liability
This book is not to be used in place of veterinary care and expertise. The authors and publisher shall
have neither liability nor responsibility to any person or entity with respect to any loss or damage
caused or alleged to be caused directly or indirectly by the information contained in this book. While
the book is as accurate as the authors can make it, there may be errors, omissions, and inaccuracies.

British Library Cataloguing in Publication Data
A CIP record for this book is available from the British Library

ISBN 978 1 872119 75 5

The illustrations throughout are the work of artist Lydia Kiernan [www.lydiakiernan.co.uk].
Cover photo © www.stuewer-tierfoto.de

Book design by Carrie Fradkin
Typeface: Adobe Garamond

Printed in China

DEDICATION

For the horses and for everyone who loves them

CONTENTS

ACKNOWLEDGEMENTS

Where do we even begin to say "thank you" to the dozens of people and horses who have contributed so much to this book? If we were to name every single one of you the number of pages necessary might require a small forest to be felled! We earnestly hope that you will recognise the contribution you've made and accept our warmest thanks and gratitude.

So many of you spared time to tell the stories of your horses, and what a deeper sense of communication with them has meant to you. Others gave precious, and hard won hours to encourage, support, and offer wise and constructive comments. We are more grateful to you than we can ever say. Your help was invaluable.

Everyone who has contributed to *What Horses Say* shares the same goal—namely to make the lives of animals a little better than before. When so many unite in a common cause, who knows what wondrous changes can be brought about?

But above all, our gratitude to the horses who have helped open the doors to a deeper understanding of the animal kingdom—especially a pony called Barney, who was the catalyst for this book.

A huge and heartfelt "thank you" to every single one of you, whether four legs or two.

Anna Clemence Mews
Julie Dicker

FOREWORD

Is it really so strange to talk with animals? People who own a dog or cat or parrot soon understand what the creature wants, when it's happy or frightened, bored or angry.

We know that animals communicate with each other and that their basic concerns are not so different from our own: food, safety, freedom, protection of the young, fighting off or evading predators, finding a mate.

We are animals and highly intelligent ones; is it really so far-fetched that someone with heightened sensibilities like Julie Dicker should be able to cross the species barrier and understand an animal when it has something important to communicate?

This book is made gripping by the number of sceptics who have been converted and have willingly told of their doubts being dispelled. "Horse whisperer" is not a term Julie Dicker likes—nor is psychic or clairvoyant. But she *is* a healer, and she seems able to see into horses' minds and hear their voices.

Since I first read *What Horses Say*, I've tried thinking, "Hello dog," when I see one in the street. It's weird, but most of them look up sharply at me and then wag their tails. I believe that now is the time to bring out the old blue coat called "intuition" from the back of our cupboards. Put it on: it fits this age better than we ever thought it would.

Joanna Lumley
London

NOTE TO THE READER

For more than three thousand years, horses have played a key part in our civilisation. Our debt to them is incalculable. For better or for worse, they have helped us change the world.

Horses have always answered our needs. But have we answered theirs? If horses spoke to us, what would they want us to know? Do the things we regard as important really matter to a horse? Or do they have a completely different view from us? What can we give animals who have given us so much?

Julie Dicker is someone who can help answer these questions—she is both an animal communicator and a healer. That is to say, she has the ability to connect directly with a horse's mind and translate their language; and she uses the gift of "healing," either through the laying on of hands, or through distant communication, to help restore health to a sick or ailing animal.

In the pages that follow, through stories that have been related to me by Julie and the horse owners who have benefited from her help, my task is to present to you what scientists regard as "anecdotal evidence" of equine emotions and reasoning powers

Over a two-year period, I carried out dozens of interviews with Julie's clients; saw their horses and wrote up their stories, checking and double-checking for accuracy. I read through more than two thousand case notes taken down by owners and riders of the horses Julie has been called to see.

To learn more about areas that might cause horses physical pain or emotional distress, I listed questions designed to get the horse's viewpoint on a range of subjects, from what made being ridden pleasant or unpleasant, to what gave them greatest happiness or fear. Julie posed these questions to a cross-section of sixty-two stallions, mares, geldings, and ponies who form a representative part of her equine clientele. The results from these surveys are included at the end of Chapters Three to Eleven under the headings, *What Horses Say* and *Summarising the Horses' Viewpoint.*

The stallions in the group included Thoroughbreds, Arabs, and Warmbloods. Some were ridden, and some were not. The mares and geldings were a mixed group of Arabs, Thoroughbreds, cobs, riding club horses, and broodmares. Most of the ponies were mixed native breeds—Dartmoors and Welsh, and a few were unbroken. The ridden mares and geldings had different roles: show jumping, racing, eventing, dressage; some simply were hacked-out and didn't compete. Some were hunted.

From many people's viewpoint, the questions were unusual ones to ask a horse. "Do you remember being separated from your mother?" "Why do you agree to let us ride you?" "Can you sense what people are feeling?" The answers were sometimes startling, often both poignant and touching.

Although there is no claim for this brief survey to be anything more than a glimpse into the world of equine thoughts and feelings, every effort has been made to present an accurate and faithful record of what the horses wanted to tell us.

Anna Clemence Mews

CHAPTER 1

The Girl Who Knew What Horses Thought

1

Julie Dicker—Communicator and Healer

If you talk to the animals, they will talk to you,

And you will know each other.

If you do not talk to them, you will not know them.

And what you do not know, you will fear.

What one fears, one destroys.

Chief Dan George

"One morning, I had a call from a girl who was getting very anxious because her horse had suddenly started spooking," said Julie. "She told me over the phone she couldn't understand it because she'd had the horse for over five years and he'd always been as good as gold. 'Bombproof,' in fact. Now, apparently, he was jumping about every time they went out for a hack and shying at everything in sight.

"When I got to the stable yard, the horse was ready and waiting, very keen to tell me what was going on. He was a bay gelding named Dan and he was thoroughly irritated with his rider. It seemed that nowadays she regularly rode him out with a friend and the two girls chattered away throughout the whole ride.

"He told me he liked the mare—he had no problems with the other horse—but he couldn't stand the way his own rider hardly paid any attention to him any more and just kept gossiping with her friend. To make her take notice of him again, he decided he'd start spooking. He'd pretend he was scared stiff of a bush or a plastic bag and suddenly jump across the road. As soon as he did, she'd stop talking to her companion and focus on him again.

"When I explained what Dan had said and that he was perfectly happy just to go out alone, or if she went out with another rider, would she please pay proper attention to him, the problem was solved. Dan went back to his usual calm behaviour."

∞

The story you've just read is true and factual, as are all the stories you will encounter in this book, although, out of respect for their privacy, the names of individuals and their horses have been altered.

Communication between humans and animals is not some childish fantasy or wistful dream. It's a real possibility. Moreover, in varying degrees and levels, it's achievable by every one of us, as Julie Dicker's experience and understanding will help to demonstrate.

Julie's approach is different from the more recent and widely recognised work of men like Monty Roberts and Pat Parelli, and the new schools of men and women often referred to as "horse whisperers." It is not based on physical or sensory observation of equine behaviour, although Julie is certainly a keen observer. She works at another level, where she is able to communicate directly with the horse's mind, acting as a bridge between horse and human. Another way of putting this would be to say that she is working with the invisible energy that surrounds all living creatures, defined loosely as "energetic material."

This vast sea of energy in which we all swim, whether we actively perceive it or not, connects us to every form of life from an earwig to an elephant, from a snail to a stallion. Some individuals are able to make this "connection" more easily than others, although it is almost certainly a dormant talent within all of us.

There are two essential aspects to Julie's work. The first part is her talent as an animal communicator, which is the ability to translate into words the thoughts and feelings that animals, and horses in particular, long for us to know and understand. It is an ability she has been aware of since childhood, and she has practised extensively—to the considerable benefit of horses and riders alike—in the ten years and more that she's been working professionally. The second part is her work as a healer—helping restore to health a sick animal. In the pages that follow, there will be explanations about both aspects of what Julie does, as well as how she arrives at the information she relays.

But first, what is an "animal communicator?" How do animals, who don't have the power of speech, communicate with us? Why aren't all of us able to "hear" them?

The language of animals, of course, is not verbal, although their understanding of our words is often at a higher level than we generally credit them. Their communication with Julie is more easily expressed in pictures—in visual images as well as sensations or feelings that she might experience in her own body. It is then her task to translate, as accurately as possible, the messages that the animal is sending.

"I have to interpret what the horse is communicating as clearly as I can. So of course, I have to put it in words that will resonate with the people I'm talking to, so they can take it on board," Julie explained. "That said, horses have very individual voices and some much more so than others.

"If I don't get a kind of inner voice or a picture, then I get a feeling of where it's hurting in the horse or in the animal, reflected in my own body.

Sometimes, it's all three but not necessarily in that order. Communication isn't something exact, and it isn't easy to explain to people what's going on. Very often the images and sensations are coming so fast that it's hard to keep pace with them."

Although communicating with animals through Julie's method might be a new concept for some, many people have been doing it for years, perhaps quite unconsciously. Today, there are ever increasing numbers of individuals around the world working in the field of animal communication and healing, adopting a non-physical approach that's been forgotten for centuries. By connecting with love, integrity, and the highest intent to universal energy, it is possible to give and receive information from the animal concerned.

Nevertheless, there are still a good many who remain sceptical about the validity of such communication, showing as it does that animals in general and horses in particular feel love, fear, anger, joy, jealousy—like Dan in our first story—and even, sad to say, guilt. In short, animals feel a lot of the same emotions that we do. Certainly, the horses that you will meet in the pages that follow appear to encompass all the emotions that make up our own human repertoire, with some even displaying a well developed sense of humour.

This leads us straight into one of the most contentious and challenging areas in science and philosophy, namely anthropomorphism—the attributing of human thoughts and emotions to animals. It is a debate that has provoked argument amongst philosophers, theologians, and scientists since the beginning of recorded thought. It will probably continue to do so for a good many years yet; at least, until science has found a satisfactory way of measuring, in an objective fashion, what emotions or abilities animals truly possess. But, to many animal lovers there is no need for argument or debate. It is self-evident.

In fact, if we are honest, we are all anthropomorphic in our relationship with animals, particularly horses and companion animals. For instance, when we say, "That horse is playing you up," we are implying that the horse is deliberately acting in a way that is unacceptable to us which presupposes a degree of mental awareness on the horse's part. He is, according to a phrase like this, conscious of what he is doing and the effect he has on us. This is certainly anthropomorphism. But used in a negative sense.

On the other hand, if we say, "He's been looking very miserable since his old stablemate went," we are being equally anthropomorphic but in a positive or sympathetic sense.

Many of the stories in this book might be considered controversial. We shall meet horses who choose the owner they want, figure out what kind of shoes they need, and know which medicine suits them best. Some are able to show extraordinary compassion for one another and for their owners. These horses are indeed capable of reason and emotions similar to our own. We are now deeply embedded in the realm of anthropomorphism.

If you have had a direct experience that has left you in no doubt whatsoever about an animal's capacity to mirror human thoughts and feelings, then crediting animals with human emotions poses no particular problem for you. But this kind of understanding—whether you call it "intuition," or "knowing," or "sixth sense," or "energy reading"—is personal and subjective. It is the opposite of science where the aim is to be impersonal and objective.

Consequently, what understandably troubles scientists is the difficulty in measuring, in an objective fashion, what emotions or abilities animals truly possess. We are forced to see animals in the light of our own thoughts and emotions, which then becomes anthropomorphism, which immediately makes it subjective, and thus scientifically unsound.

The stories that you are going to read are profoundly anthropomorphic and depending upon your point of view, they might be regarded in several ways. You might consider it absurd that a horse like Dan could be jealous of the attention his rider was paying to someone else or show an accurate understanding of his own emotional needs.

Conversely, based on your own experience, you may find the horse's intelligence and understanding quite believable. It rings true to you. Or you might look at it through the lens that many are inclined to use, which is to consider it *might* be true but you require more hard evidence.

Considering it might be true but more evidence is needed is certainly a fair point of view. The whole issue of animal consciousness and what it implies is moving to the forefront of a good many scientific minds. The study of animal behaviour, also known as ethology, taps into an endless labyrinth of research that touches on anthropology, artificial intelligence, ethics, metaphysics, philosophy, psychology, psychoneuro-immunology, quantum physics, and theology. It is a complex, multi-layered, multi-threaded arena.

In the final chapter, there will be a closer look at the problems that anthropomorphism poses for the scientific community together with the difficulty in finding clear definitions for the ways in which animal communicators work and why information is often received in such a variety of ways.

Although communication is an important part of what Julie does, she defines herself primarily as a "healer."

"When I was a little girl," said Julie, "I always knew when an animal was sick. Nobody in our family thought it was unusual. It was just accepted. It wasn't until I was about thirteen that I realised not everyone saw things in quite the same kind of way. I can still remember telling a friend that her cat wasn't very well. She asked me how I knew. I told her it had just said so. It was obvious. I could feel the cat's pain in my own body, and I wondered why they didn't do something about it because the poor creature had awful stomach ache. The friend said, 'You're weird,' and looked at me in a really odd way. It was her look that upset me more than anything she said. I realised I'd made a wrong move—that suddenly I was different. So I just put my hands on the cat and stroked it.

"I came home and cried, but I didn't tell anybody. You don't want to be different from everybody else when you're a teenager. After that, I learned to listen and keep quiet. But, when I was with animals that belonged to my friends and they weren't well, I'd just put my hands on them. Most people didn't know what I was doing, so it was okay. I never told anybody what the animals said."

A straightforward definition of healing is simply, "to restore to health." One of the earliest forms of healing was traditionally referred to as the "laying-on of hands." However, the term "healer" is often used today in all sorts of contexts. In the movement widely called "New Age," healers often define themselves through a multiplicity of names and disciplines: "Spiritual," "Psychic," "Magnetic," "Colour," "Crystal," "Therapeutic," "Reiki," "Radionic"—there seems to be no end to the list or to the complex web that has been woven around the word "healer."

"To me," Julie said, "the essence of all healing is love. Healing is simple and straightforward. If you're genuinely giving love to an animal or a person, then you're giving healing, no matter what you call it. Everybody can do that. And everybody does. Some people do it all the time and never realise it. But for sure, everybody is a healer at some point in their lives, however they define it."

Although Julie works directly with the mind and the spirit of the horse, there is nothing "airy-fairy" about her methods. She has a professional, matter-of-fact approach to both communication and healing.

Clients are asked to take notes and given a pen and book in which to write them. They keep the top copy, which also includes details of the date, horse's name, age, height, and colour and she keeps the carbon. Before she begins, she makes an assessment to pick up the general personality pattern of the animal. Then, she makes her way down from the poll, to the mouth, and then on down the neck, withers, shoulders, front legs, back, hindquarters, and hind legs—first one side and then the other. As she works, she's giving healing and often talking, relaying to the owner what the horse is thinking or feeling.

"It's quite difficult for me to separate communication and healing," said Julie. "When I first encounter a horse sometimes, there's a lot going on in his head and he wants to tell me things right away. Sometimes, he doesn't have much to say but is in pain and that's what I have to sort out first. Every horse is different. But, if I'm called to see an animal, it would be very unusual if it didn't need healing. Although, sometimes just being able to tell me what the problem is can be healing in itself, as in the case of Dan. He wasn't in pain. He was just fed up!

"What am I actually doing when I give healing? Well, that depends. Essentially it is giving unconditional love. Real, deep compassion, if you like. Physically, I usually have my hands on the horse's body, although it isn't always necessary. Sometimes, I do a little light manipulation or use light pressure on certain points. I am guided wholly and completely by what the horse wants me to do. I don't impose anything on him or have a rigid routine that has to be followed. The horse dictates the session. I am only there to help him."

∞

Horses have carried us, hunted with us, pulled our loads, ploughed our fields, provided our sport, and with courage and gallantry, gone into battle and died with us.

Few people could doubt that the horse has been, as the Arabian proverb puts it, "God's gift to mankind." Physically, humankind has had a unique relationship with these extraordinary animals. Horse and rider have a physical closeness that is only equalled when we are in the womb or engaged in the act of making love. Given the horse's virtues of strength and speed, their incredible beauty and grace, and their patient, enduring natures, it's hardly surprising that for many of us they hold a magnetic attraction.

Nor is it surprising, given our history, that communication with the horse is possible at a more profound level than is sometimes believed. To achieve a different degree of understanding with your horse, or indeed with any animal, you don't have to be a special age or sex or colour. You don't need expensive equipment, elaborate rituals, or even years of training.

You need love as your starting point. It is the essential and vital ingredient. To love, you need to add patience and an open mind, with the courage and willingness to follow your own intuition. What can then be achieved might astonish you.

If some of the stories you are about to read appear challenging, perhaps the words of Gautama the Buddha may offer encouragement:

Believe nothing because a wise man said it
Believe nothing because the belief is generally held
Believe nothing because it is written in ancient books
Believe nothing because it is said to be of divine origin
Believe nothing because someone else believes it
But believe only that which you yourself judge to be true.

CHAPTER 2

Hearing the Silence, Seeing the Invisible

Communication and Healing in Action

Betsy

One summer morning in a quiet tree-lined field, Betsy, a dark brown mare, is standing at the gate, ears pricked. Elegant, sleek-coated, she has the alert, ready-to-race look of the good Thoroughbred. The object of her attention is a pretty bay filly being lead towards the field. The filly dances about impatiently, eager to be free of the rope and headcollar. There's a swift moment of mutual nose sniffing as the two horses meet. The girl slips off the filly's headcollar, stands back, closes the gate, and walks away. The horses are alone together.

Freedom! The filly is off in a flash, a blur of mane and tail, a comet with four legs and stretched out neck. She's gone once round the field before the brown mare even gets into gear. Betsy breaks into a trot but surprisingly, looks stiff and awkward. Her new companion is moving as though jet-propelled. Nostrils flared, brimming with youthful excitement, she gathers herself up for another burst around the field. Betsy trots slowly towards her. The two horses almost meet. They could collide, and Betsy tries to avoid the filly. She swings to the left—and so does the filly. Her shoulder bangs into Betsy's hindquarters. The mare throws all her weight on her front legs, jarred into a muscle-wrenching stop.

By mid-afternoon, Betsy doesn't look much like a born-to-race Thoroughbred. Her head is down, she's hobbling, and is in considerable pain. Her pain is evident to her concerned owner, but unfortunately, the mare has no way of explaining what has happened.

"I have to say," said Sarah, "that when Betsy came in, I felt desperate to see her in such a state. I had no idea what she'd done to herself."

Sarah is Betsy's owner. She is a no-nonsense, down-to-earth lady who breeds Thoroughbreds for flat racing and has done so for over twenty years. Horses are as much part of her life as breathing.

"I tell you, that mare's cost me a fortune. An absolute fortune. From the moment she went into training, there was just one thing after another. First she went lame in one leg, then in another—she worked her way around all four.

"Then she got laminitis. Oh, and by this time her back was obviously giving her trouble. I was just about at my wit's end when our vet came up with a suggestion. He said he thought I should take Betsy to see some 'healer woman' who was doing an equine clinic. Well, I can tell you I was pretty sceptical. If anybody else had suggested it, I probably wouldn't have taken much notice. But he was a vet and a good one, so I thought, 'Okay, I'll give it a go.' As far as I was concerned, it was absolutely a last resort. I'd spent so much on this mare, trying to get her right and keep her sound, I thought I might as well try one more thing, however unlikely it seemed."

The "healer woman" was Julie Dicker.

"I liked the look of Julie," said Sarah. "She seemed sensible enough but I was wary. I didn't think that anyone could really pick up what went on in a horse's mind. Anyway, she seemed to know what she was doing. She stood at Betsy's head for quite a while. Then she began picking up a lot of Betsy's hot spots and went round and put both her arms around the mare's hindquarters. I was a bit surprised but Betsy seemed quiet enough and Julie went on telling me about various problems the mare had had. She was absolutely right so far. Then she began laughing.

"She said she often saw things in pictures. What she was seeing now was a box of old fashioned toffees with a bluebird on it. Frankly, I thought she must have gone absolutely potty. I wanted to say, 'Let me out of here, I've made an awful mistake. This woman is completely daft.' But Julie just shook her head in a puzzled kind of way and went on about this 'bluebird' and the box of toffee. She told me she didn't understand it herself, it made no sense at all to her. But because Betsy kept sending her this picture, Julie knew it had some significance.

"So I stood there, racking my brains and trying to think what a box of toffees with a bluebird on it could possibly have to do with a Thoroughbred mare who was so lame she could hardly stand up. I vaguely recalled that there was a firm who made toffee and used a bluebird as their trademark. But it still seemed ridiculous to me. Then I remembered I'd got a yearling filly we hadn't christened properly yet. We just called her the 'Bluebird filly' because she's out of a horse by that name. So I told Julie we had a youngster that went by the name of Bluebird. But that was the only connection I could make. She asked me if Betsy had ever been turned out with the filly.

"Then it hit me like a ton of bricks! Of course she had. When Betsy had gone lame with laminitis, I'd been told to put another horse out with her just to make sure the mare moved around a bit more. The Bluebird filly was a lively little thing full of beans and seemed just what Betsy needed to get her going.

"As soon as I told Julie this, it all began to click into place for both of us. Right away, Julie said, 'Yes, that's it—that's how it happened.' Apparently, the Bluebird youngster had gone galloping around the field like mad, and poor old Betsy hadn't been able to get out of the way fast enough, and they just collided.

"It was extraordinary. I was amazed at the way the information came through. And what was even more wonderful was that Betsy got better so fast. She hadn't been sound for nearly nine months. But two days after this session, she was out in the field, trotting around just as smoothly as you please."

∞

In Julie's world, this is the kind of thing that happens day in, day out. For her, it's neither remarkable nor extraordinary, yet from a conventional viewpoint, Betsy's healing was certainly unusual. Sarah herself, although astonished at the time, is now accustomed to working with Julie and accepts that such swift healing can often occur.

"I was over the moon," said Sarah, "but of course I was surprised by the speed of Betsy's recovery. Now I just think, 'Well, that's healing for you.'"

"Betsy," said Julie, "was in terrible pain. I remember walking round to the front of her and getting such a violent feeling of tightness all across my chest, as though I'd picked up something really heavy. It made me feel quite sick. I was conscious that the colour was just draining out of me, and I knew Sarah could see something was going on. She'd never met me before and I could tell she was concerned.

"I thought to myself, 'Oh no, she's going to think I'm totally cracked.' I asked Betsy what was happening. I wasn't sure if it was her pain I was picking up or whether I'd suddenly done something awful to myself. Anyway, right away she answered, *It's me. I've done the splits and torn my muscles.* So I told her she didn't need to make the pain so strong, because I could sense it anyway.

"Then the mare asked me to put my hands around her backside. So I went to her hindquarters and stood there with my arms around her. Something very powerful happened then, a profound release from the mare. There was some kind of instant healing and I knew she was going to be fine."

There are aspects of healing that are constantly surprising and unexpected. No one ever knows exactly what form it will take, nor what the effects will be, nor how long before the pain disappears. Julie herself certainly never makes any claim as to what the end result might be.

"Sometimes," Julie said, "it can be difficult to interpret what an animal wants. Then you just have to persevere. At first, I couldn't get what Betsy was trying to tell me. I picked up her pain immediately and I did what she asked me to do, which was to put my arms around her hindquarters. I suppose I was hugging her. Honestly, to feel that much pain in another living creature can only make you do everything possible to ease it and take away the agony.

"When I'd asked her to show me how she had got injured, how she'd come to be in such a bad way, to be given a picture of the lid of a box of toffees with a bluebird on it didn't seem to make any sense at all. You might say, 'Well, why on earth weren't you just shown a bluebird?' My answer would be, 'Quite frankly, I don't know!' I don't make up the rules and my job is to translate the images that I get as best I can. It may have been to make what I was doing more difficult and therefore more convincing to Sarah who was certainly sceptical to begin with.

"Very often you just have to hang in and try to work out what the animal is telling you. If all you want to do is help it get better, sooner or later, you'll understand what it is trying to say."

Happily for Julie, the degree of discomfort she experienced when Betsy was trying to tell her how she felt didn't last long. When she's sent a "pain" message by an animal, it's usually quickly received and quickly dispersed. But it gives an immediate and very physical understanding of the animal's discomfort.

"Of course, the healing starts as soon as I connect with the animal, whether I'm there physically or not. For me, healing is the really important part of the work I do. That's what counts most. You don't need to know everything about the animal or pick up every word it's saying to give healing. For me, healing is sharing a space where unconditional love can flow. So when people ask me, 'Are there limitations to healing?' my answer is always the same. There are no boundaries and no limitations, only what you place on yourself."

This may well be why animals can often respond more dramatically to healing than human beings, for they place few roadblocks on the way to recovery. Unconditional love, though, is the first essential, whether you are intending to give healing to an animal or whether you are trying to deepen your level of understanding through working at a mental level. To approach the arena of either communication or healing without it, is about as much use as trying to drive a car with no fuel. Large amounts of patience are needed, too, as well as an open mind with the courage and willingness to follow the intuitive path.

Of course, loving an animal is a wholly natural thing. So natural in fact, that most of us never give it a second thought. It's easy enough to do when a horse does everything you want it to and responds beautifully to your every wish. But, when he's having a bad mood or has just deposited you on the ground, "unconditional love," as everyone knows, can be a tad more difficult to maintain.

"In my experience," said Julie, "If you want to communicate, the first thing to do is nothing. Nothing at all. That in itself is quite difficult for a lot of people. But it's where you have to begin. You just need to stand quietly and observe. Send out as much love as possible but don't try and force the door open. The animal may not be in a mood to talk just when you feel like it. You must respect their wishes in every way.

"But, if you try, in a loving and respectful fashion, in its own way and in its own time, things between you and that animal will start to open up. Animals will answer you in a way you will both understand. It may be the simplest of gestures. Or, you might send them a telepathic message, asking them to indicate yes or no. Make it something very easy to do. And, do it over and over again, so that the horse knows and understands. Keep it simple.

"People approach the business of communication with so many preconceptions and ideas in their mind. But you've just got to eliminate all your thoughts and expectations, and for most of us, this is the hardest part. If you can achieve that, and keep the love unconditional, it will open the doors to deeper communication."

Looking again at the second aspect of Julie's work, healing can be as simple or as complex as you care to make it. Using her definition that, "If you're genuinely giving love to an animal or a person, then you're giving healing, no matter what you call it," we are all able to do this when we love our animal—in very much the same way that a loving parent naturally responds to the needs of a child who's hurt or wounded.

∞

Another aspect of what Julie does is a form of "seeing the invisible," or tuning in at a distance to an animal who is in need. This, too, is a talent we can all access, in varying degrees, through regular meditative and spiritual practice. The following story illustrates how this ability, wisely used, can bring help and comfort.

One Sunday evening, Julie was sitting in her living room, feet up, leafing through the papers and enjoying a few hours of rare peace and quiet. Then the phone rang. The caller was a distraught young woman who reported that her friend's daughter, Rosy, had been out riding with another little girl. Rosy had fallen off her pony, who had bolted and disappeared into a wood. Although Rosy had returned home unhurt, accompanied by her friend and *her* pony, Rosy's pony was missing. Please, could Julie find him?

Julie listened carefully, then without any hesitation, began to speak very quickly giving directions as if to someone on a treasure hunt.

"As soon as I tuned in," said Julie, "the picture I got was the pony with his head down, still wearing all his tack, alive and well. I wanted to know exactly whereabouts the pony was. Then, I got a picture of the pony walking along and me walking beside him. In my mind, I counted the paces as I walked. The information I got through this was for them to go back to where the child had fallen off, turn left for about a hundred and fifty paces, and then turn right for another hundred paces and finally, a hundred and fifty paces left again, and the pony would be near a mineshaft."

It was too dark for a search party to go out that night. Before they set off next morning, Julie received another anxious call to see if she had any fresh information. Once again she listened attentively.

"There's been no big change," she said, "this time the pony's shown me a picture of a clearing with grass. He's very frightened and absolutely exhausted, poor little chap."

Off went the searchers, desperate to find the missing pony who was clearly by now very distressed. Later that day there was another phone call. This time, there was general rejoicing. They had followed Julie's instructions to the letter and the pony had been found just where Julie said he would be.

"Apparently," said Julie, "when they found the pony he had his head slightly down, which is how I'd seen him. It was because his reins had got caught on a branch and he couldn't put his head up. The funny thing was, though, all the time I kept getting this picture, quick flashes if you like, of a grey pony. I thought it was a bit odd, because I'd been told Rosy's pony was a roan. But somebody said that Rosy's friend had been riding a grey pony. Of course, then I immediately understood what had been happening. I realised the information I'd been receiving must have come from the other pony who had been out on the ride, the grey, because Rosy's little roan pony was too scared and exhausted to communicate clearly.

"The grey pony who'd come home safely was helping him out. But, that kind of thing does happen quite often. If a horse can't communicate directly with me, sometimes a stablemate or close companion will do it for him."

As well as the whole process that some call "remote viewing," there is an added dimension to the secret world of the animal's mind. Animals, as Julie has learned, can communicate on behalf of other animals.

"Very often, there's a horse that's more knowledgeable than the rest, and it will relate its friend's problems. But it's not just horses. Sometimes a dog will tell me what's the matter with a horse or a cat, and sometimes it's the other way around. Some are able to give you answers with no trouble and for others it's quite difficult. Usually, I find horses the easiest to communicate with, and they're generally the ones that take over as interpreter for another animal, say a dog or cat. It's basically individual, though. Some animals are knowledgeable and articulate. Some aren't."

Whenever this kind of inter-animal information relay happens, it's often a source of amazement to the onlooker. On one occasion, a young man was asking if the chestnut mare that he'd just brought to the stud was happy to be put in foal.

"Oh yes," said Julie. "She's fine about that. But her friend, the bay mare back at home, doesn't want a foal. It probably won't happen either, no matter how often you take her to the stallion."

The young man looked visibly surprised, not to say shocked.

"How do you know that? How do you know I've got a bay mare that's the very devil to get in foal?"

The bay mare in question was at his farm, some thirty miles away.

"Her friend here," Julie nodded towards the chestnut, "she's just said so."

"Well, I never!"

∞

As the box of toffees with a bluebird on the lid demonstrated, animals often send their messages through visual symbols or pictures, invisible to the physical eye. Whilst the ability to see the invisible is a gift that we all possess, particularly as children, it's something that can get blunted, or even deadened, as a child grows older; especially so if in adulthood there is unwillingness to exercise it or even to trust it.

However, "intuition," the art of knowing without the knowledge coming from our rational, reasoning mind, is something everyone uses regularly, day in and day out. It's the warning that tells you, "Slow down, there's a car coming round this bend on the wrong side of the road," long before you could possibly see it or hear it. It's the sudden awareness of what someone is going to announce, before he's even opened his mouth. Or, thinking hard about a friend who's been out of touch for years—then getting a phone call from her that evening. Or, simply "just knowing" that a certain event is going to happen long before it does. Intuition is a natural and integral part of our daily lives. In fact, the human race probably couldn't function without it.

Because intuition appears to act outside the range of our five physical senses—sight, sound, smell, taste and touch—it's sometimes regarded with disbelief or suspicion. It's intangible, irrational, illogical, and doesn't seem to be under the control of our reasoning mind. Intuition acts as a "sixth sense"—but like every sense, it has many levels.

We readily accept that on the physical plane, some of us are born with naturally good eyesight or a well-developed ear for music. Others have an extra keen sense of smell or taste. But practice in any of our natural physical senses will make them even better and the same is true of our intuition—or sixth sense.

The sixth sense that links us closely to the invisible world is a gift everyone has, but does not necessarily recognise or use to the full. Julie, and many other sensitives throughout the ages, do so, and have been doing so since the day they were born. It's as much a normal part of their everyday life as it is for a master of wine to recognise whether a sip of Bordeaux came from the north or south bank of the Garonne or a conductor to hear a flat C in the woodwind section.

If we choose to, through working patiently with love, integrity, and the highest intent, the inner world that belongs to us all can be accessed and developed.

What the animals say is the secret world many of us would like to enter. Just imagine what it could be like if we really knew what horses felt and thought. Suppose they told us exactly what they enjoyed doing—or, not doing. Suppose they told us what really hurt or frightened them. Do they think we're a pretty useless bunch they just have to put up with? Or, do they love us? And, do they know how much we love *them*?

If we could all enter the horse's world, would it thrill and delight us? Or, would we be shocked by the suffering many of them endure? There are many questions, and some possible answers will be offered, as the stories unfold of just some of the remarkable horses Julie has met.

We thought you'd like to know horses' reasons for letting us ride them, what kind of rewards they prefer, what really scares them, what causes them pain, and what makes them happy. Above all, we wanted to know what they needed most from us. Some of the answers were what you might expect. Others were very surprising.

CHAPTER 3

Basic Instincts

3

Close Attachments, Separation, and Grief

Suki

The foal frolics around the mare, nudging and nosing until she finds the source of food. The mare stands patiently, occasionally putting back her head to give the foal a gentle push on the rump—just a reminder not to overdo the food intake or suck so hard the mare's teats are made sore.

The foal is growing well. Full of bounce, she finishes feeding, gives her head a little shake and trots off to investigate the contents of an empty bucket by the gate. The mare watches her for a moment, decides her offspring can't get into any mischief and begins to look for food herself. This is her first foal, and she's now carrying a second.

The mare works vigorously over a patch of the field, nipping the grass cleanly down with a thoroughness that would do credit to a lawnmower. Every few minutes, she lifts her head to check on the foal, who's still playing with the bucket. The mare wanders along the edge of the field. She'd really like something else to eat—grass is good, and so are the buckets of food— but there's something missing that she'd dearly like. The blackthorn bushes are just coming into flower. She would normally display caution, nipping the leaves neatly, folding back her lips and using her teeth as precisely as any two-legged person might use a pair of scissors. But the smell is so tempting she forgets that the blackthorn can be treacherous. The mare takes a generous mouthful of the leaves, swallows, and then gives a sudden choking cough.

Something painful has caught in the soft flesh of her throat. She coughs again, harder, trying to dislodge the sharp, scratching object. She tries to eat a little grass but that hurts too. The only thing that seems to ease the pain is constant coughing. That, and the presence of the foal who rubs up against her flanks, nuzzling her in a concerned and puzzled way. She waits patiently to be brought in, still coughing, still making every effort to get rid of the pain in her throat.

Lynne is a professional horsewoman who's owned, bred, and trained competition horses for years from an immaculate stud in the heart of Devon. Over the years, she's frequently asked Julie to talk with, and give healing to, a good number of her horses.

"I think that since I've been working with Julie, I've become far more aware of the horses' body language, but not just that—their whole personality, too. The more you tune in to them, the more you understand. On the other hand, though, the more you tune in, the harder it becomes because you can't let them down by doing the opposite of what they want. If they say, 'Don't feed me oats, it makes me feel really bloated,' then you just can't do it. It also makes it tougher because you have to pay more attention. Once, I might have waited for more obvious signs if there was any hint of a problem. Now, I pick things up far more quickly. Of course, you reap the benefits because the horses work better and they're happier."

When Suki, one of her broodmares and a big bay Warmblood, was brought in coughing, Lynne went into action immediately.

"Suki was a lovely mare, very easygoing, but definitely greedy. Her first foal was about four months old and she was in foal again. Everything seemed absolutely fine. Then, she came in from the field coughing like mad, as though something was stuck in her throat."

To begin with, Lynne assumed she had choke or an object stuck in the throat that was pressing on the oesophagus or windpipe.

"But, we soon realised it was something more serious than that. Our vet, Jonathan, X-rayed her and she was scoped but she was losing weight dramatically."

The scope, or endoscopy, is performed in a similar way to the procedure in a human being. Suki had to have a tube put down her throat with a small camera attached to see if there was any obstruction. Despite the best veterinary attention, the mare was still unable to eat any quantity of food and continued to lose weight.

"Over a period of three weeks, she went from a fat mare with a weight of around 600 kilos to a skeleton of a mere 300 kilos. She would stand in a corner of the stable, very tucked-up and trying to swallow and then vomit, as if she had grass sickness, although that diagnosis had already been ruled out. We were getting desperate."

When Julie came to see the ailing mare, Suki relayed some surprising information.

"The first picture," said Julie, "that Suki showed me was of a blackthorn bush. She was biting into it and eating a mouthful of leaves. I saw a picture of the inside of her throat looking red and swollen, as if something was stuck to it, like a needle threaded in.

"I asked her if it was a thorn and she said, *yes*. Then I questioned her and asked why on earth she'd been eating the blackthorn. I immediately got a feeling of hunger, and she said, *to stop me feeling like this*, and she showed me a picture of a brittle kind of bone. I got the sensation of my teeth being very loose and I remembered that the only time in my life I'd had that feeling was when I was pregnant."

Whenever she's faced with this kind of information, Julie has to make a sensible interpretation. Discussion with the owner often leads to a useful conclusion and, most importantly, one that is helpful to the horse.

"When Julie and I talked about it," said Lynne, "it was clear that Suki had developed a craving, just as pregnant women often do. Why shouldn't pregnant mares do the same? We then figured that through the picture of brittle bones that Julie had been shown, and the sensation of 'loose teeth,' what Suki probably needed was extra calcium. Perhaps it was this that she was trying to get through the blackthorn leaves. It's certainly the case that as an in-foal mare, with a first foal at foot, her body had huge demands for calcium. She was getting this in her feed but was unable to metabolise it sufficiently. So we immediately treated her with calcium and continued it for about three months.

"We had Suki scoped a second time by another veterinary surgeon," Lynne continued, "but on this occasion it was under a general anaesthetic. The true damage was revealed. She had septic ulcers. The camera found little pockets of ulcerations down her throat, all oozing puss. It bore out exactly what Suki had relayed to Julie. By mistake, Suki had evidently swallowed the prickly thorns as well as the leaves and a thorn had perforated her oesophagus. This in turn had gone septic.

"The vets decided to keep her alive on strong antibiotics and by pumping liquid food every two hours into her stomach through a stomach tube. They said the foal she was carrying would probably be aborted due to the stress and intense drug therapy. On the other hand, they considered that if the mare was put down, which was a possibility that we discussed with the veterinary team, there wouldn't be a foal at all. It was a deeply distressing situation. There didn't seem to be any ideal solution.

"Not surprisingly, Suki's milk began to dry up and she wasn't able to feed the foal very much. Luckily, the youngster was now on some hard food, so she didn't try bullying her mother for more milk. Julie was coming most days to give Suki healing. After about five weeks, the mare began to show a little interest in the foal's food."

"I remember," said Julie, "asking her if we should take the foal away, if she should be weaned. Suki was absolutely clear about this. She said that the foal gave her something to live for and she showed me a picture that said very plainly that if we took the foal away, she would die. So we all just had to keep going. Round about the time she began to take a look at the foal's food, she said she wanted the stomach tube taken out. We were all a bit concerned about this, and I asked her again and again if she was sure and she was quite definite."

"We were very anxious about taking out the stomach tube," said Lynne. "We said, 'Okay, if you really want the tube out, we'll do it.' But, we gave her a good feed through it first. Once it was out, we would make up stud cubes for her but turn them into a kind of porridge so it was easy for her to swallow and digest. The foal was still with her because that's what she said she wanted. But after a couple of days of eating her 'porridge,' she told Julie that she didn't want the foal around any more."

"Yes," said Julie, "she was as clear about that as everything else. She suddenly said to me, when I was giving her healing, *take her away—I've had enough now.* When they did, there was absolutely no fuss from either of them—mare or foal. It was obviously the right time. I've seen so many examples, over the years, of the way that the mares behave and how they show it when they're ready for the foal to leave them. I think that when they're ready, probably the foal is too. Then there's no drama or trauma."

During this long period of intensive nursing, Suki had become deeply attached to her human carers and the bond between the mare and Lynne had deepened.

"She would get very worried if I wasn't about and every time I was just ready to go out in the evening, she would develop colic. So, I wouldn't go. A huge amount of effort had gone into saving her, and it seemed a small enough sacrifice to make. Suki was ill for about two months but she got well and eventually gave birth to the foal she was carrying. It was a colt. Right up to the moment he was born we had no idea if he would be deformed. But there he was, a normal healthy foal. He was on the small side, but he had a spectacular physique. We called him Wonder! We kept him entire till he was about eighteen months old in order to give him a good start. He is absolutely marvellous and completely lives up to his name."

The long suffering and patient mare, Suki, went on to produce four more foals and is still, according to Lynne, "One of the greediest horses I've ever known."

∞

Jonathan considered the case of Suki to be very unusual. A second generation veterinary surgeon with a farming background and more than twenty years experience of equine and large animal practice, he has considerable respect for Julie's talents and thinks that as individuals, we probably only use five percent of the abilities we possess.

"If I could find a way to unlock the ninety-five percent, I'd be very pleased. I suppose I could say I have a similar gift to Julie, but only to a degree. Certainly, I'd like to find a way of speaking to my patients every time I see them!

"Frankly, I was amazed by the way Suki accepted it all when we were treating her. It was remarkable the way she tolerated it. I asked myself more than once if we were doing the right thing to keep her going, or whether we should be putting her down. Julie reckoned she put up with it because of the foal. Certainly, with hindsight, I think it's rare for a horse to recover to Suki's extent."

Suki's programme of recovery didn't simply follow conventional, orthodox, veterinary treatment, essential though it was, but also took into account the wisdom and preferences of the mare herself.

"Quite a few horses crave obscure things when they're pregnant," said Julie. "I remember one mare who had a lot of stomach trouble but when she was given slippery elm, it settled down. Until then, she'd been eating bark off an elm tree. She knew what she needed. I am certain that all horses know exactly what they need when they need it, but it's not always easy for them to get the message across."

From the horses' standpoint, of course, what they need as "food" includes not just grass, hay, oats, or any of the thousand-and-one commercial mixtures or subtle variations on nature's provisions, but also the simple herbs of the hedgerows and meadows. The medicine cupboard once available to them has vanished, long since fallen victim to chemical sprays and agricultural machinery. This may well be why horses take such pleasure, as you'll see later, in dandelion leaves, or in Suki's case, the tempting taste of the blackthorn. Mares do have a profound sense not only of what they need, but also what is right for their offspring. Their highly developed protective instinct indicates that "mother knows best" as far as most broodmares are concerned.

∾

Caro

It is very quiet inside the stable. The mare is lying down, her sleeping foal beside her. Safe in her familiar home environment, the mare is confident enough to stretch out and even to doze lightly. Suddenly, she hears the sharp scream of a fox. The mare is instantly on full alert, scrambling to her feet immediately to guard her sleeping foal. She is so preoccupied with the need to protect her offspring she doesn't consider anything else. As she struggles to her feet, a hind leg shoots out and catches the foal sharply on the hock.

The foal gives a little squeal. This agitates the mare still more. By the time she is on her feet, ready for any necessary action, the vixen is silent. The night is quiet again. She bends down to nuzzle her offspring, pushing her nose against the bruised hock, nudging her to get up. The filly does so with difficulty, just managing to feed, although when she moves around the stable she appears quite lame.

"Caro," said Lynne, "is a mare who is really good with her foals. She's always been an excellent mother. But, when her filly foal was about ten days old, we noticed she had a slightly swollen hock and was a bit lame. There seemed no apparent cause but we wondered if she might have joint ill, so we asked Jonathan to take some blood samples."

"Navel" or "joint ill" is a disease that sometimes occurs in newborn foals, lambs, and calves. It's a form of infection that is often triggered when the umbilical cord is cut but it also can attack the joints and cause swelling, stiffness, and pain. If the swelling around the joint bursts, it releases fluid that contains shreds of fibrinous matter. Results of the blood samples showed that the fibrinogen levels were high because of damage to the joint. The cause of the damage was another matter.

"If the foal had got joint ill, the fibrinogen levels in the blood sample would be raised because of the infection," Lynne explained. "So, I wanted Julie to come and have a look at the mare and foal and give them both some healing."

"When I asked Caro what had happened," said Julie, "she showed me a picture of her getting up very quickly. She said she'd heard a noise that had startled her. Because she got up so fast—being so startled—she'd accidentally leaned on the foal's hock. I saw this picture of a very thin bone, like a chicken bone, very porous. Over it was something that looked like gauze but with big holes in it."

During the years that Julie has been interpreting horses' messages, she's come to devise a code, or a way of translating certain images. For example, when she receives a strong image of a solid-looking beef bone, she interprets that to mean that the animal's bone is healthy. When she gets a picture of a thin bone or one that appears brittle and full of airholes, almost like a sponge, she generally finds it associated with a bone-related ailment.

Julie came regularly to give the foal healing. Then one day, Caro made a specific request.

"She sent me a picture," said Julie, "of the stable next door and said she wanted to be moved there. I had the impression of a very beautiful, healing energy there that seemed to envelop you. It was clear the mare felt the foal would recover faster in that box."

"When Julie passed on the mare's request," said Lynne, "I was very happy to do what she wanted. In fact, I'd already noticed that in the corner of that particular box there seemed to be a comforting kind of presence."

As the healing progressed, Julie got different images of the damaged hock.

"When the foal was getting better, I got pictures of the holes in the gauze getting smaller and closer together, until finally, it was a single, closely knit covering. It was about this time, I think, that Caro asked to go into the other box, and the foal seemed to do even better when we moved them."

A week or two after the mare and foal had moved to their new quarters, something occurred that neither Julie nor Lynne had ever encountered before.

"Julie was giving the foal healing," Lynne explained, "her hands on the foal's hock. Suddenly, there was this extraordinary sound of a heartbeat. 'Bump, bump'—it was as loud as if there was a radio in the room, with sound coming out of a set of speakers. We looked at one another in absolute amazement.

"The mare was very calm and snoozing away peacefully. And the foal was lying down and perfectly happy. There was no stress, nothing frightening going on, no loud noises. Well, none, except for this amazing sound of the heartbeat."

"It was quite awe inspiring," said Julie. "I remember how we both stood there for several minutes, just looking around to see where the sound could possibly be coming from. It really took a while for it sink in that it was Caro's heart thumping away. When I finally asked her what was happening she told me that she was simply reassuring the foal, letting her know that everything was okay. She was always a very protective mum.

"From the pictures she sent me, it seemed that mares and foals recognise each other by heartbeat, their own individual heartbeat. If the foal has strayed away from them in the dark, they'll send out a loud heartbeat to help it find its way back. It's a signal to give reassurance."

Over the days that followed, the times when the loud heartbeat occurred were fewer and fewer. Within about five weeks the foal was completely healed.

As these stories suggest, the power of the mother-offspring bond should not be underestimated. In each case, the maternal instinct played an essential role—in one case, in the mare's recovery, and in the other, the foal's.

∞

Becca

But suppose there is a sudden rupture, an abrupt breaking of the bond before the time is right?

Josie is a veterinary surgeon who is not only a highly experienced horsewoman but a specialist in equine medicine. She has never underestimated the sensitive nature of the mare-foal relationship and relates the story of Becca, one of her mares with whom she formed an especially deep bond. When Becca's first foal died during birth, Josie paid great attention to the mare's emotions.

"Of course mares grieve. Why shouldn't they? If a foal's born dead or dies at birth, it can't just be ignored. The bond is already there. Every horse is an individual and from the mare's point of view, grieving is as important for her as it is for any human mother. I know most people just want to get rid of the foal as fast as they can. It upsets them and they want it out of sight. But, that's so unfair on the mare."

Josie and her husband were deeply sensitive to Becca's mood and left the foal in the stable where it had been born. Becca was unwilling to leave the little filly, even to go outside and eat. Josie took care not to disturb the vigil and left the mare quietly in the stable, standing guard over her dead offspring. For a day and a half, she brought food in for the grieving mother.

"On the second night, when it got dark and everything was very quiet, I heard Becca go outside for a bite of grass. If anything disturbed her, anything at all, she'd panic and bolt back into the stable, oblivious to whatever was in her way. I started to put some food outside to encourage her to go out, but the drive to get back in and stand by her foal was too strong. You could literally feel the mare's grief and sense of loss as you walked in the stable. It made me cry—it still does today, when I look back on it."

Anxious to make sure the mare didn't lose strength and condition, Josie and her husband decided the best thing to do was to carry the foal outside and into the field.

"I suppose some people would find it grotesque to take the foal out, but it was what was needed for the mare's sake. You could see exactly where she'd been grazing. There was almost a perfect circle around the foal."

It was summer and by the third day it was obvious that the foal could no longer be left with Becca.

"We arranged for a chap to come out with a digger bucket so that we could bury it. I noticed that were already a few hummocks of grass over the little filly. I think Becca had tried to bury it herself. Mares will very often do this if they get a chance. They'll try and kick earth or paw at grass to cover it, or straw if they're left in the stable. Anyway, just before the digger came, I told Becca it was okay and she could leave the foal now. Then she walked away. She was ready to let it go.

"Later that day, I put her in with the other mares and she just went back to them very peacefully, and started eating. She was very easy to get back in foal again. When mares lose a foal, especially if you don't let them grieve, it can be very difficult to get them in foal again. It's not just a question of hormones and follicles and ovulation. It's about their whole mind and body balance. Looking back, I felt privileged that Becca had allowed me to share her grief. I feel the strongest bond ever with her, which continues to this day."

Alvin and Lilo

It isn't just mares and foals who form deep relationships, as was very evident when we visited Peta and her husband, Leo, who have reared livestock and bred point-to-pointers on their farm for more than twenty-five years. They related a poignant story of how one of their geldings became mother to an orphan filly.

Several years ago, one of their best broodmares, April, gave birth to a filly foal named Lilo. Because April foaled earlier than they had expected, she was still out in the field, rather than brought in for the night. Consequently, the attending midwife was a dark brown, retired point-to-pointer called Alvin. Alvin was thirteen, a year older than April. They had grown up together and had always been friends.

"From the very beginning," said Peta, "Alvin took a great interest in Lilo. He was always nearby, always keeping a watchful eye on both mare and foal. If the weather was bad, we'd bring April and Lilo into the stable at night. We had to bring Alvin in as well and put him next door to them. When Lilo was very small, if he couldn't see her over the partition he'd get absolutely frantic."

But on a cold evening in early November, when Lilo was barely five months old, tragedy struck. April was taken ill with colic. It was sudden, unexpected, and fatal. Within hours, the vet had been called out twice, the first time to administer painkillers, the second, a short while later, to put April down. Lilo was motherless. But Alvin, with extraordinary sensitivity, took the mare's place and assumed a major role in Lilo's life.

As a consequence, the young foal's distress was, Peta said, "A lot less than anyone might have expected in those sort of circumstances, although

I have to say, all our horses have always simply doted on foals, the geldings just as much as the mares. The fan club queues up at the gate to watch a foal. When Lilo went by, all the geldings would drool over her and want to speak to her as she trotted past."

Alvin never left Lilo's side for a second and their devotion to each other was almost tangible. His patience with the young filly was exceptional, by any standards.

"Lilo even tried to suckle, at first," said Peta, 'but he just pushed her away gently and moved himself out of range."

Lilo and Alvin are still the closest of companions.

"This summer," said Peta, "we turned them out together with one of our oldest mares. At the beginning, Alvin defended Lilo as if he were a mother with a newborn foal. He kept himself between Lilo and the other mare and it was several days before he relaxed his guard. We want to introduce one of this year's foals to Lilo so she'll have a young friend, as well. When the day comes that the two have to be separated, even if it's only when Lilo has to be backed, we shall certainly do it with the greatest care."

Through Julie, Alvin and Lilo were asked what was the most frightening thing that had ever happened to them. Lilo answered, *losing mother.* And Alvin said, *losing sight of Lilo.*

∞

Enlightened breeders, nowadays, make a big effort to carry out the weaning process gently. There's certainly a lot less of the old-fashioned way of abruptly separating mare and foal, often first shutting up the foal in a stable with both doors closed, so it wouldn't harm itself by trying to jump out. Timing appears to be crucial, and as we saw earlier with the mare Suki, there was a point where she couldn't bear to be separated from the foal— and then a moment where it was exactly what she wanted. Finding the defining moment can make a world of difference as Malcolm, a breeder of outstanding Arabians, knows very well.

"Before the foals are weaned, it's critically important that they bond with another creature—human, or animal—so that when they're separated from their mother, they have someone to go to. The biggest problem, very often, is that the foals haven't made either a human or another horse relationship before they're taken from their mother. If they feel confident there's a world without mum, then it's not such a shock when it happens. When we do have to make changes, it's important that as many things as possible stay the same. If a child has to go away for the night, it's much better if he takes a favourite toy. With the foals, it's a similar thing. It's far more comforting for them if they go into a stable they already know, where the smells of their own mother are still present."

Equally, if separation only occurs rarely, that too is a cause of equine anxiety. Malcolm is very aware that for many, parting is certainly not a happy affair. Horses, he considers, will do almost anything, as long as they have a friend to accompany them through the problems in their life.

"There's no doubt in my mind that friendship between horses is very important to them. On one occasion, I was buying a mare from another stud, and the owner suggested that I bring along one of our own mares of a similar kind and temperament so that she could befriend the new arrival. I took a mare called Lena with me and she was introduced to Phoebe, the mare I was buying. The two of them had a chance to get acquainted before they both came back together to the farm. From the moment they stepped out of the horsebox, they were inseparable.

"I am quite sure that bonding with Lena before she came made a tremendous difference to Phoebe. It was probably the only thing that enabled her to feel she would live through the whole business and be safe."

On the matter of friendship, one of the most touching answers came from a stallion who had a particularly difficult life and had been considered to be both dangerous and volatile. However, once settled with an owner who understood the horse and could deal with him, his personality changed. When Julie asked him whether he had a special friend, he said, *yes, Carl.*

Carl was his owner.

But horses, unlike cars, are seldom able to have the benefit of "only one careful owner." Most of them have a number of owners, and relatively few are fortunate enough to spend their lives with the same human or equine family or stablemates. Separation from family and friends is an almost inevitable part of a modern horse's life.

∞

The Bay Stallion

The stable is comfortable and a generous size, with plenty of hay and water and a bed deep with straw. Air and sunshine are freely available through the open top door. But inside, the bay stallion is restless. The straw is churned into little furrows as he circles around the walls, pausing at each side for a second as though trying to remember why he moved there. With powerful hindquarters, a strong, well-set neck, and a fine head, he's a handsome example of his breed.

When a small group of people approach the door, he hesitates for a second, then wheels around and moves towards them, pulling back his ears and glaring. One of the group moves nearer the half-open door, but not so near that equine teeth could meet the fragility of human shoulder. There is no talking, no chitchat, just silence.

The figure closest to the stallion moves still closer. The stallion pauses, as though considering his next move. His ears are flicking back and forth, more in indecision than in any desire to listen. If he were free, he could run away. But the four, solid walls contain him. His eyes hold an expression of sadness and profound bewilderment. Then they change, swiftly, to hostility. He flattens his ears hard back against his neck, pulling open his lips to snap his teeth. The gesture is designed to be menacing and the body language is easy to read, "Stay away from me. Stay away, or I may do you harm."

The figure outside the door remains quiet, unmoving. The stallion seems a shade calmer. His ears have come forward, although his body is still tense and stiff. It wouldn't take much to send him spiralling out of control, a muscular bundle of high-octane energy in a box. No one outside the stable has moved or spoken.

Yet suddenly, there's a visible and dramatic change in the coiled-up horse. The stallion drops his head, as though too weary to hold it up a second longer. He begins to lick and chew, his tongue moving around his mouth, his jaw relaxed. They are the classic signs of a horse who has decided neither to run nor to fight, but to stay and listen.

Julie had posed a question that brought a dramatic response from the stallion, so dramatic that it was impossible to ignore.

"I asked him if he remembered being separated from his mother. He said he did, and that he wasn't ready to go. He was weaned early, then put on a boat from a country a long way away. It made him very unhappy. He's never been able to forget it."

His owners confirmed that he had indeed come from "a long way away" and, in fact, had been brought from northern Europe by boat and train. Although he had had a travelling companion, another young colt, he never seemed to settle happily in his new home. Despite good treatment and considerate handling, he remained a difficult and restless horse.

Whether the bay stallion would have been so troubled if his weaning had been less abrupt, no one can say. However, it certainly seems that a gentle separation, sympathetically handled, is likely to pay dividends in the future behaviour of any colt or filly.

WHAT HORSES SAY

What *do* horses feel about separation from family or friends, or about the death of another horse? Julie asked fifty-five of our sixty-two horses and ponies:

Do you remember being separated from your mother?
Seventy-six percent, a clear majority, didn't remember anything about the event. It drew no particular reaction and they seemed to have no recall or painful memory. Twenty-four percent of our group did remember. For these horses, the remembrance was distressing. Their response was *wasn't ready to go.* What they actually relayed about their weaning was sometimes very poignant. The bay stallion's response was echoed by others, who said things like *one minute she was here, then she was gone.* Some reported that it all happened *far too fast,* and they had been *shut up in the dark,* and had *screamed a lot.* The speed of the event, the suddenness, the fact that the animals were not in any way prepared for it, left its mark. Some who remembered would not talk about it.

How do you feel about being separated from your companions?
Fifty-eight percent, a narrow majority, were not unduly bothered by it. It looked as if they could cope with separation, especially if they were going off to do something interesting or exciting that they enjoyed.

Forty-two percent were anxious or apprehensive when they were separated or had to leave their friends. In horses who had enjoyed the benefit of close companionship or herd life, the anxiety seemed greatest. From what appeared later, it looks as if it is the actual uncertainty that is distressing. Their reaction might be described as saying, *what's happening? Why is it happening? This happened before and something bad took place.*

Are you upset by the death of another horse?

Eighty-nine percent of the group gave an unequivocal *no*. The majority appeared to take a straightforward view of the matter. They did not seem to register distress at the idea, and there certainly seemed to be a remarkable acceptance of death.

The other eleven percent, however, grieved for close companions. It may be that these horses were not given sufficient warning of the event. Other evidence suggested that being able to bid friends farewell might be as necessary for horses as it is for us, if grief and suffering is to be lessened.

SUMMARISING THE HORSES' VIEWPOINT

Close Attachments, Separation, and Grief

The emotions of grief and loneliness appear to affect horses far more than we are inclined, or sometimes want, to believe. Domesticated horses rarely, if ever, have the chance to remain within or even close to their own family group. Few horses live their lives in the home and hands of the individual who bred them. We take it for granted that they are unlikely to have any contact with the stallion who sired them. We also assume that separation must be made not only from their mother, but from their companions, where the bonds of friendship often go deeper than we imagine. To be separated from their own kind, at our command, is a fact of horses' lives.

However, the manner in which we do it, the sensitivity that we display to their needs, and the time we take over it, appear to have a profound effect on the their well being.

Insensitive weaning and separation from companion animals obviously doesn't appear to affect every animal adversely. However, the fact that most of the horses questioned did not remember the event, doesn't necessarily mean that they suffered no emotional distress. Julie finds that "blocking-off" is very common among animals who have suffered trauma. She never pushes them to convey anything they don't want to reveal. The choice is always theirs alone. They decide what, when, and how they wish to relay information to her.

She has also observed, over the years, that a young horse taken early from his mother or family group, who perhaps hasn't had a lot of interaction with other horses, often requests an "older companion." Horses certainly need to learn from other horses, not just from human beings.

Although deep friendship with their human companions is and can become very important as the stallion who belonged to Carl clearly showed, the friendship of their own kind plays an essential role in horses' happiness and sense of security. Sometimes, as every horse owner knows, this can be a problem when certain stablemates have to be separated, even if it's only to go for a hack.

Although the majority of horses questioned could cope with separation, it was evidently because they were confident that they would return to their companions. In these circumstances, they are not too fussed. Equally, when they in turn are left behind, they know their friends always come back, so they feel unworried.

Some learn to cope with separation better than others, whether it is leaving their mother or their friends, although we'd certainly be kidding ourselves if we said, "Oh well, they don't really mind." A lot of them do mind. Some, like the unhappy bay stallion, mind very much.

As for death, or the ultimate separation, horses appear to be more pragmatic than we are, and have a higher acceptance of it. Although the majority of horses seemed unperturbed, it doesn't alter the fact that they are capable of grief and a sense of loss when a close companion has died. Further evidence suggested that when a horse had the opportunity to say good-bye to a companion, the loss was easier to accept.

The distress shown by Becca at the death of her foal shows how deeply equine emotions can run. It is an area we need to acknowledge more respectfully and with greater compassion than is often the case.

CHAPTER 4

Love At First Sight

4 Rewarding Partnerships

Lucy

The market is concrete and cold steel. Wind creeps along the back of the bay mare, making her flatten her ears and tuck in her tail. Stood alone between the metal bars of the pen, head lowered, she dimly remembers other markets she's passed through. Hands pushed her into cramped trailers, other hands led her into unfamiliar stables. Voices were usually loud, sometimes kind, more often rough. Bodies and breath held the aroma of burned-out cigarettes, stale beer, and the grease of unwashed dishes. Yet, somewhere in the mare's hidden thoughts, lay a memory of something sweeter, something gentle, a scent of hope. When the half-remembered scent drifted to her across the concrete aisles, she raised her head for a second, nostrils quivering. But the scent moved further away.

Suddenly, strange hands pulled her into the ring, into a circle of blurred faces and voices buzzing like angry bees. Several times she stumbled but each time was sharply, impatiently tapped into a faltering trot. The auctioneer's hammer fell with a final brisk note.

Alone again in the pen, she was slowly aware that the scent, the good, sweet scent was coming surprisingly close. She concentrated all that was left of her strength. In a final burst of energy, she stretched out her neck and grabbed the

jacket that smelled of June hay, golden straw, and kindness—real kindness—
between her teeth.

   Exhausted, she could do no more.

Pippa is a woman who listens to horses and has done so all her life. For over twenty years, she's run a large teaching and livery centre in the West Country. Her farming background has given her a comprehensive knowledge of animal behaviour, born of keen observation and plenty of hands-on experience. The soft voice and gentle manner are combined with a clear-sighted view of what an animal might need and how best that need could be fulfilled. At her first meeting with Julie, she was sceptical about communication with animals, despite her own sensitivity and deep-rooted intuition.

   "I'd heard of Julie, and I first asked her to come here several years ago and see a horse called Minnie. There was nothing wrong with the mare, but I was curious to know if she was still rideable, as she was quite old."

   Pippa got a clear and unequivocal answer—yes, Minnie could be ridden. Pippa then wondered which saddle would be most comfortable for the horse and brought a selection out to test on her.

   "This was the most fascinating thing. We'd put three saddles on the wall in front of Minnie. When we tried the first one on her, she was like a savage horse. She made a sort of 'Agggghaha' scream. I was astonished by her reaction. The second saddle we tried got a less violent response, but she told Julie she didn't want that one. Finally, when we tried the third saddle, she went 'Ahhha,' and Julie said, 'That's the one.' I found it all amazing, and I was hooked."

   Pippa has never lost touch with her own intuition, which has always served her well in her relationship with animals.

   "I've often bought horses over the phone. I don't need to see them. I seem to know immediately if they'll be right for me or not. Oh, occasion-ally, one has gone a bit wrong, but that's really been because their early training went haywire somewhere along the line. It simply means you have to start again. There are definitely horses that respond to me and find me—and I seem to know instinctively which ones to go for."

This ability to respond to an animal asking for help gave an Irish cross-bred Shire mare a second chance in a life that had literally dealt the horse some cruel blows.

Once a month there's a horse sale at a market near Pippa's. It has the usual collection of dealers looking for a bargain, country people on a day out, horsemen and women, day-trippers, and the just plain curious. What's on offer on any given day can range from clipped-out Thoroughbreds to woolly children's ponies.

Horseboxes and trailers loading and unloading, sudden loud noises, crowds of strangers, and dozens of animals herded into holding pens, all con-tribute to a charged and hurried atmosphere. Markets, whether for horses or livestock, are uncomfortable places, despite constant efforts to improve wel-fare and handling. Stress is inevitable for animals and humans, and the heart-break potential is enormous. Pippa's trip to market one chilly winter morning turned out to be more of a mercy mission than even she had realised.

"I often go there, not necessarily to buy but to meet people and some-times just to see what's around. You never know when you're going to pick up something you can help. I was walking down the aisles of horses in this cold, penned market, knowing that sometimes, however much compas-sion you might feel, a horse just isn't for you. I noticed this big bay mare and felt a sense of pity for her. Then, she went in the ring and I didn't see her sold."

But the bay mare had also noticed Pippa.

"When I came back down the aisles a bit later, I walked by her and she just grabbed hold of my clothes. Literally. I stopped and looked at her face and body. She was thin and racked with pain and oh, such a sad horse. I turned to my husband, and said, 'That does it. She's coming back with us.'"

Pippa went off to find the man who'd bought the bay mare and immediately struck a deal with him.

"Then we went to load her. Oh Lord! As soon as we walked her on, I could see she was absolutely crippled and I thought, 'Oh no, what have I done—you'll never get up the ramp.' But, she did. It took us a long time. I realised we couldn't shut her in the compartment, she'd just fall over, so we put her 'long ways' in the back of the horsebox so she could balance."

When Pippa and her husband got back to the farm, it was almost as difficult to get the mare out as it had been to get her in.

"It took ages to get her down the ramp. I had a long look at her and thought, 'I've made a huge mistake. I'll be surprised if she lasts the night out.' It was pathetic. The poor soul couldn't lie down, her back legs went into spasm and she shuddered and shook, then took one step forward. It was so painful just to see."

Pippa decided that she needed to know more about the mare's history. She asked Julie to come and look at the horse, now called Lucy, to discover what more could be done to help the courageous animal.

"It was obvious that she was a lovely creature. She wasn't a difficult mare—you could see that. There was something so touching about her. I felt sure Julie could put me on the right track to help heal her. And I was sure Julie could give her healing and that would do a lot of good. Somehow or other, we got Lucy into the indoor school but every step caused her pain. She kept shuddering as she walked. She was terribly bent to the left, just like a banana."

Julie began to listen to Lucy's story. Bit by bit, she relayed it to Pippa.

"I knew before I started," Julie recalled, "that this was going to be something utterly heartrending. It was like stepping into a deep well of pain and bereavement, yet the mare was desperate to share it with us. The whole atmosphere around us was of love and peace. There was a sense of deep compassion."

Pippa was moved to tears.

"I remember," she said, "how I kept on saying 'Oh my God, oh my God.' I'd already noticed that in the left side of her neck there were two severe dents, one upper and one lower. It was as if someone had taken a huge needle and threaded it through the flesh. I couldn't understand what had caused such marks. Lucy told Julie she'd been 'naughty,' and they'd driven a stake through her neck. That poor, poor mare. As if that wasn't bad enough, sometime later, they'd put a headcollar on her and attached a rope to her tail so her head was forced back towards her tail in this awful, crippling shape. She was left tied like that for days. No wonder she was bent like a banana."

Julie, as she remembered later, was quite bewildered by it all.

"I didn't understand what I was relaying. I really didn't. I'd never heard of such things. I didn't think it could be true. It was completely out of my league. I was in tears and I said to Pippa, 'Have I got this right?' and she just nodded and said, 'Carry on—I'll tell you in a moment.'"

Pippa knew that tying a horse nose-to-tail was not uncommon in parts of both North and South America in the last century. It was considered a suitable method of subduing a horse who showed too much spirit or, because of his size and strength, frightened his trainers.

"But the heartbreaking thing," Pippa continued, "was that the poor animal never knew what she had done to be treated like that. Whatever 'naughty' may have meant, she had no idea of what it was. Julie said it was just something the mare was told by the people around her."

However, having a stake driven through her neck and being tied nose-to-tail was not the end of Lucy's troubles. Possibly as a result of her being considered difficult to school, she was put in foal. The mare relayed to Julie that she'd been frightened and forced by a large stallion.

"Then," said Julie, "I remember that she moved her head back in the direction of her tail and lifted it and showed me a picture of stitches."

"It's not unusual," Pippa went on, "to stitch down the perineum after a mare has been served. It's done to make sure she holds the foal, particularly if the mare is a bit floppy."

But Lucy was not being cared for in a highly observant stud farm. When foaling time came, no one had the thought or consideration to remove the stitches.

"The foal literally had to rip itself out. One side of her bottom expanded, and a bit of the vulva, too. You could plainly see that her backside was deformed on the right. Honestly, it was just horrendous what that poor horse had suffered. After that, she'd been shipped to England, wrecked and crippled. She'd already been to Salisbury Market and no one wanted her.

"Julie gave her a lot of healing and Lucy said she wanted her to come back in two weeks, which she did. When Julie came the second time, she worked on the right hind leg, and Lucy said she was going to be okay now and Julie didn't need to come again. That in itself was amazing, that Lucy should recover after only a few treatments."

Such a brutal start to the mare's life could easily have made her the sort of horse who hated human beings and would never ever trust one again. But remarkably, and miraculously, that wasn't the case.

"After Julie's final visit, Lucy just went on from strength to strength. She'd do everything you asked her to with such enthusiasm, and she loved taking people out on the moor. Sometimes it was quite hard to pull her up. You'd have to say, 'Lucy, will you stop!' My husband took her to a meet and she simply had a ball. In the end, he had to turn back because he just couldn't hold her. It's wonderful and miraculous how she's turned out because few animals could have had a worse beginning."

Sometime later, the mare was ridden occasionally by a local veterinary surgeon who confirmed that the scars on Lucy's neck were almost certainly made by a stake. She remarked, "There were deep grooves along her neck—you could still feel the channel where some object had been driven under Lucy's skin."

Although Lucy was now well and happy, Pippa had always felt the very best place for the mare would be a home with one dedicated owner. Some months later, Pippa had a visit from a young woman whose mare had just died. She gave Pippa "chapter and verse" about the kind of horse she was looking for and wondered if Pippa knew of one that might fit her detailed description.

"It was amazing because she totally described Lucy. I went to see where she would be living and it was just heaven sent. The place was excellent and she is a like-minded person who cares about horses in a very holistic manner."

Lucy went off to a new home where she was warmly welcomed by the other residents, as well as her new owner.

"As soon as we put her out in this lovely, big, fifteen-acre field, one of the young geldings called to her as if he'd always known her. They're the best of friends—he protects her and loves her. It's very touching."

Pippa has always regarded horses as her friends, but since her experiences with Julie, an even greater understanding has emerged, which continues to grow and develop. She feels that working with Julie has increased her own level of intuition and ability to receive clear communication from a horse.

"One day, I was quietly lungeing a new horse in my outdoor school. I suppose I was getting quite involved with him, really getting into his world rather than staying in my own. I became aware that he had started to go a bit short on the offside. All of a sudden, I felt this dreadful pain in my right hip. I wondered if it was me, or the horse. I thought, 'My God, if this pain isn't in my hip, the poor horse must have a bloody awful pain in his.' So I started shaking my leg and moving about. I got quite flushed and it was really painful. Then, just as suddenly the pain went, and at the very same moment, Jack began moving smoothly again.

"Of course, I've always cared about animals but perhaps the deep feelings I have now were not fully awakened until I met Julie. Now that I really know how much horses are capable of communicating, I look at them in a totally different way. I'm sure I always communicated with them in my own fashion, but I'm beginning to find out how to do it a lot better. I've become much more aware of their body language and the communication they give back to me.

"I listen to their answers because they will most certainly give us answers if we allow them to. Unfortunately, most of the time we're too arrogant to stop and listen. The gifts that horses have given to us, to human beings, make me feel very humble. They're an ancient and noble race, and I think mankind has been served by them more than by anything else."

On that cold day in the market, Lucy had made every effort to reach Pippa, to be noticed by her and send a signal that would be recognised and understood.

"She knew," said Julie, "that Pippa was a woman who would be able to help her. She could sense that Pippa would treat her with dignity and respect and do things gently."

Perhaps Lucy had tried before, in other markets, to choose the owner she wanted but had met no response to her efforts at communication. Sometimes, horses have to make signals that are unmistakeably clear.

∞

Barouche

Although the black horse was in less than perfect condition, it was still easy to see how handsome he had once been. He stood apart from the rest—the other horses in the field keeping a respectful distance that seemed to suggest he should be approached with caution. He was edgy, watchful, waiting attentively until he caught sight of two girls. Turning only to pull back his ears at another gelding who had started to follow him, he began to move purposefully towards the gate. The first girl drew back slightly as he approached. The second stood very still. He put his head over the railing and dropped it in front of her. In quiet surprise, she gently rubbed his neck. Eyes half closed he, too, stood still.

Dawn has ridden all her life—Pony Club activities when she was younger, and later, training as a British Horse Society instructor. Nevertheless, she was surprised to be chosen by Barouche, a horse who had rejected, and been rejected by, a score of others in a troubled and often painful life. A handsome, black Thoroughbred, he had been bred and flat raced in France, and later, brought to England to run as a hurdler.

"I'd seen him," said Dawn, "at the yard where he was being kept. To be honest, I thought he had a really vile temperament. He was certainly a very nice-looking horse, but if you went by his box, he'd come at you over the door.

"I didn't think too much more about him until a friend said to me, 'You know that black horse? He's going to be sent to the knacker's.' I went out in the field, just to have another look at him, really. What happened was really quite surprising. He came over to me and put his head in my arms. It was extraordinary. I felt I had no choice but to try and buy him.

"The dealer who owned him was asking for £700. It was much more than I could afford, especially for a horse who not only had a very strange temperament but was lame as well. I offered him the 'meat' price, which was about £300, roughly what he would have got at the knacker's. He phoned back the next day and said I could have him for £350, but he wanted the horse gone from the yard as quickly as possible. I don't really think he thought much of him. Later on, I found out why.

"Anyway, he loaded without any trouble and I brought him home. I could see that one shoulder blade was more advanced than the other. He was clearly lame, but I already knew that. I decided the best thing to do would be to give him three months rest out in the field and see if he would come sound.

"I brought him in regularly and handled him a bit. He was difficult—very awkward to groom, and nobody wanted to go in the stable with him. He'd let fly at them from both ends. He was all right with me. But with anyone else, he'd have a go with the front legs, and if that didn't work, then he'd lead with the back."

There were, of course, immediate practical problems with such an immensely wary and frightened horse.

"There was no way," Dawn continued, "you could treat him for any medical reasons. I knew he needed his jabs, but I wasn't sure how it was going to be done."

Dawn contacted Josie to do the deed.

"Josie," said Dawn, "is such a knowledgeable and experienced horse vet that I reckoned she'd be able to inject him all right. When I phoned her, she said, 'I know that horse—I won't be able to get near him.' That wasn't too promising. Believe me, Josie isn't faint-hearted or easily put off. It was pretty likely we weren't even going to get close enough to sedate him."

However, there was no doubt that Barouche had to have his tetanus and flu injections, and both Josie and Dawn prepared for the ordeal.

"I'd tied Barouche up outside the stable. But, as soon as Josie drove into the yard and got out of her car, he went absolutely mad. He was totally aware and knew what was going to happen, even from the whole length of the yard away.

"We just looked at each other, and Josie said, 'Look maybe *you've* got to do this.' So while Barouche was busy lashing out at Josie—he was concentrating all his fury directly at her—I managed to get the syringe in."

Josie was very aware of the difficulties that Dawn was having with the horse and suggested that she attend a clinic she was running nearby. Julie would be there, too, and Dawn could see how Julie worked and decide whether she could help with Barouche's problems.

A few weeks later, Julie came to have a session with the troubled horse.

"Oh, he was lethal," Julie recalled. "His eyes were out on stalks, his nostrils were flaring, his legs were going, and I was thinking to myself, 'How on earth am I going to get near this?' But we went in, and Dawn put a halter on him and when I started to touch him he settled down quite quickly."

Julie was able to give Dawn a good deal of information, not only about Barouche's past injuries, but also why he had adopted such a hostile and aggressive attitude.

"He had a problem in front of his withers," said Julie, "and a really big problem in his left shoulder that had been caused by a severe fall when he was racing. He'd come down hard on it, and on his neck as well. He'd also been punched really hard in the nose, which gave him a dull ache above both nostrils. He used to get very scared at the start of races and try to run his jockeys off against the rail. His saddle didn't fit and at the back of his ribs on the right hand side, he'd been hit or kicked until he bled."

"It was an appalling list of things," said Dawn. "His skin was so sensitive it wasn't always comfortable for him to be groomed, which was obviously why he hated it so much. I never tried to clip him. He'd just put his head in the corner if he even heard the clippers, so I never bothered him with it.

"Barouche also told Julie that he'd had a long journey in a horsebox and didn't have any water, which fitted in with him coming over from France to England. The poor animal had had a terrible time. It wasn't surprising that he'd become so difficult. Who could blame him?"

After Julie's visit, life continued to improve for Barouche, and with Dawn's continuing patient and understanding care, he began to settle down.

"He gradually got so he was pleasant to ride out on the road. He was absolutely one- hundred percent in traffic. I took him hunting and he was super. I could even lead my young daughter out on him."

But, a year or so later, he suddenly went lame.

"One of the vets, not Josie this time, came to see him," continued Dawn, "and suggested putting him down. The physiotherapist couldn't get anywhere near him. By the time Julie came to give him healing, he was hopping around on three legs. She told me he'd hurt his shoulder by putting a foot in a rabbit hole. After that visit, he was much better and walked back to the field. Julie came two or three more times, and he gradually got better and better so I was able to start riding him again. We hunted for the next two winters and he went really well."

But Barouche's problems were not entirely over. As a more-than-twenty-year-old horse, who'd had a tough life, it was not surprising that his periods of lameness grew longer and more frequent. By the time the following summer rolled around, Barouche had been lame for five months. Dawn's devotion to the horse ran deep, and she was unwilling to put him through any veterinary procedure that was likely to cause him more distress.

"When we got to winter again, he still wasn't sound. I'd had him for three years and I know he'd been happy. So I made the decision to do what was best for him. Barouche deserved a dignified and peaceful end to his life."

When the moment came, that was exactly what he had.

WHAT HORSES SAY

To learn more about what horses feel makes them happy, our group, all in good homes now, was asked two questions. There were sixty-two different answers, many of them highly individual.

What do you enjoy most about your life?

Thirty-two percent of the horses, including most of the stallions, considered that *being busy* was important to an enjoyable life. Responses included things like *showing off, having a say*, and *performing*. It was clear that certain horses adored going to shows, being ridden out, and generally having plenty to do.

Nineteen percent of the group found great pleasure in *one-to-one attention* and being *pampered* in one form or another. Being shown love through grooming, stroking, and having the full attention of a human being, was a big part of happiness for these horses.

Eighteen percent regarded *being part of a herd* as important. These horses needed to *feel secure*, and being part of a herd or group gave them that security.

Thirty-one percent gave unusual replies as to what made their lives enjoyable, pointing out the highly individual nature of the equine race. These answers included things like *being a mother, freedom, being fed, not doing a lot, seeing the sheep*, and *not having a headache*. Only one old mare no longer seemed to find enjoyment in life and said she was *tired*.

What rewards do you enjoy most?

Forty-five percent of the group, the greatest response, came from a single, unqualified answer: *praise!* Horses need to be told, in no uncertain terms, through words and actions, that they have done really well and that we're absolutely delighted with them. Some added that they wanted a *caress*, as well.

Thirty-one percent considered that *hugs, cuddles, and caresses*, or plenty of tender loving care and attention were the best reward for their efforts. They wanted to be *stroked gently* and *caressed*.

Fifteen percent of our group were satisfied with food as a reward.

Nine percent did want food, but food alone was not enough and to be *praised* or *caressed* was wanted as well.

SUMMARISING THE HORSES' VIEWPOINT

Rewarding Partnerships

The world had been a tough place for Lucy and Barouche, until they found themselves in homes where they were understood and appreciated. For a happy life, horses value activity, as Lucy demonstrated when she relished going hunting, and as many other horses we questioned bore out. If the activity, however, is one that causes pain or fear, as evidently was the case for Barouche during his racing career, then a horse's temperament can turn very sour indeed. Especially so, perhaps, if a vital element for happiness is missing—namely praise for a job well done.

Companionship and security is important, too, as was also demonstrated in the last chapter.

Praise was an absolutely essential ingredient in a rewarding partnership, and we shouldn't be surprised to learn how highly horses rate it. Maybe this is a powerful indication of how important it is to remember to *tell* them when they have done something wonderful. Horses don't just understand our gratitude and appreciation—they actively need it. Whether it is the words themselves or whether it is the relaxed, cheerful energy that the rider gives off when a request or a movement has been successfully executed is not clear. But, without a doubt, the warm tone of voice in which praise is normally given is not only clearly recognised it is also extremely important to a horse.

Horses that wanted stroking and caressing as rewards for their efforts, did not highly rate being "patted," however affectionately it might be intended; this type of hearty slap on the neck—so often seen at shows and events—is even disliked by some horses. Interestingly, Arabian breeder Malcolm has a strict, "no patting" policy with his youngsters. He feels patting is stimulating rather than soothing, and from what the horses in our group indicated, this may well be the case. A stroke or caress, on the other hand, is like a mother's tongue—the first comforting, physical contact between mare and foal, even before the foal begins to suckle.

Although food is often considered the perfect reward, the horses in our group did not place it in the same category as being praised or stroked. Horses may relish titbits, but evidently not as much as many human beings are inclined to believe.

From the horse's viewpoint, a rewarding partnership should include an activity that the horse genuinely enjoys performing, gentle physical affection, and, above all, warm-hearted, enthusiastic praise.

CHAPTER 5

Horses Who Know Their Own Minds

5

Freedom to *Choose*

Garth

Change was coming. He knew it, and new people came to ride him. People smelled different to him—all of them different. There were a few, just a few, who smelled so reassuring he wanted to stay close to them. Others—whew, back off, get away, avoid them. Sometimes he would brace himself and go very stiff because it was not wise to kick, or bite, or rear, even though the only thing he really wanted to do was move away way from the unpleasing scent. One rider always sat gently on his back, so lightly, and still it was a pleasure to carry her. The scent of her kept him calm and happy.

He had observed that hobbling horses were not ridden—that pulling one foot higher than the other, using only three legs and not four, brought a day without work. He also observed that horses who did not walk or trot straight seemed unwanted. So, when riders came whose smell didn't please him, he hobbled and stumbled until a person who understood the pattern of his thoughts arrived at last. Then, he showed her exactly what he wanted.

By and large, horses don't have a lot of opportunities for choice. They're not usually asked whether they'd like to hang out in the field or stay in the stable. Or, whether they'd rather canter down the right hand bridle path or the left. Or, even canter at all. If they do have a stab at making their preference clear, the chances are it won't be enthusiastically received. However, a magnificent, chestnut gelding named Garth succeeded in making several clear choices but only through a complex series of events.

"It's a long story," said Alan, "and it began when I first saw Garth one November morning. He was turned out with a flock of sheep and we had to trudge across a couple of fields to get to him. His breeder, who was quite tiny and a bit elderly, whistled to the sheep. Suddenly, around a bend in the field thundered this great, big, hairy chestnut. Up he came at full gallop, caught sight of his owner and us—then immediately changed pace to a short, collected canter and slid to a halt in front of us. He never once lost his balance. It was quite dramatic, especially as his owner, who couldn't have been more than five feet tall, barely came up to his chest!"

Alan has been a professional horseman for over ten years and is a British Horse Society Instructor. Essentially an event rider, he competes on his clients' horses as well as his own. He also spends a large part of his time teaching, and travelling to instruct pupils from seven to seventy in a range of disciplines, including dressage, show jumping, and cross-country riding. His experience and knowledge in dealing with a wide variety of horses and riders on a daily basis has given him plenty of insight into how horse and human normally communicate.

Alan immediately recognised Garth's athletic abilities and could see that although he was young, untrained, and roughed-off, here was a horse with real potential. He was exactly the sort that any professional horseman would be glad to take on, knowing that with careful schooling he would be a good investment of time and money. The gelding was just five years old when Alan began his education.

"I think to use the words 'broken' or 'breaking-in' is only appropriate because most people understand what you mean. I tend to use 'training' or 'educating' because they come closer to what you're doing. Although, even training makes the whole business sound as if you're asking the horse to behave like a performing dog. It's like saying, 'Here's your command, and this is your response.' But, that's not the way we want it to be. I really prefer the word 'educate' because that allows room for the horse to think and problem solve—to use his mind as well as his body."

By the time he was six, Garth was beginning to jump, hunt, and compete in local dressage. Then, a puzzling sequence of events occurred. He started going lame, first in the foot, and then in the shoulder. Veterinary surgeons X-rayed and nerve-blocked his lower leg, but nothing showed up. There were intermittent periods of being sound, then, the lameness would reappear, seeming to move up-and-down the leg, between foot and shoulder. As soon as the shoulder appeared better, the lameness reappeared in the foot, with this frustrating cycle continuing for about eighteen months.

Garth was by now seven years old and it began to look as if his potential was never going to be realised. Vets' bills were mounting fast and the horse was becoming a very expensive investment. Alan decided to ask Julie if she could discover what was going on.

"Julie had been a huge help to us with another horse and by this time I had a lot of confidence in what she told us. Although, I have to say that in the beginning, I was very suspicious of her! My wife and I had had some experiences, not related to horses, which had opened our minds to a wider dimension. Looking back, I think I was more spiritually aware than I knew. But, I was definitely wary. I'd already met someone who could 'talk to horses,' and although I was prepared to accept this could be done, the person I met gave me inaccurate information. So, at our meeting with Julie, I decided I wasn't going to open myself up to it or get carried away.

"I have to admit," Alan continued, "that in a very short time, she described specific problems that this particular horse, Barty, had undergone, mentioning things that only I knew about him. So I started to relax. Then she made an extraordinary remark. She said, 'Barty says he'd like to have another gin and tonic.' I could feel myself absolutely recoiling and thinking, 'Damn, I've been done again.' But, when I stopped to consider for a moment, I suddenly remembered what had happened.

"Barty had done so well at the Windsor Three-Day Event. We were absolutely thrilled and we'd wanted him to join in the celebrations. So we'd poured him a little gin and tonic and put it in an ashtray, which I must say he lapped up with considerable enthusiasm.

"Looking back, I think it was Barty's way of giving us a specific memory to help us accept Julie's work. I also think it was a remarkably brave thing for Julie to relay to us. Anyway, from that moment on, I was prepared to accept the accuracy of her work. For me, it was confirmation that there was another, deeper dimension I could tap into."

Julie arrived late one evening to have a look at Garth and see if she could discover what was going on.

"She immediately began to demonstrate with her own body exactly how the horse was moving," said Alan. "She indicated this contorted, twisted position, which is just how he moved. Then, she came up with several things about what was happening, for example, that as a yearling, he'd run into a gatepost, badly bruising his left shoulder. This made a lot of sense, as of course, the shoulder would affect the balance of the foot and then the shoulder would hurt when the balance of the foot was correct— and then he'd put his back out, and so on."

Julie worked on him, and after further treatment, his back and shoulder began to improve considerably, but he still seemed to have problems in the foot. Julie asked the horse what he thought would help.

"This is where we began," Alan explained, "a really interesting three-way process. Julie is very good at getting horses to distinguish between what they want and what they need. When she came back with the answer that Garth wanted his shoes off, we both knew that wasn't a very good idea. His feet would almost certainly break up. We then we had quite a long conversation—Julie, Garth, and me. It was a real discussion about what Garth would find best for him. I knew that we had to get the balance of the foot exactly right. In the end, very much with Garth's input, we came up with a good solution and were able to design the kind of shoes he wanted."

The farrier wasn't aware that the shoes he was asked to fit had been designed with the horse's help and cooperation. But he confirmed that they should do the trick, and a design was produced that gave protection to both front feet.

"We got it right in the end," said Alan, "but very much because of Garth's understanding and Julie's ability to interpret it."

In the short term, the gelding's troubles seemed over. That is, until the problem of temperament bubbled up. Garth and Alan did not seem to be compatible, but Alan couldn't explain why.

"I simply don't know what it was, but somehow or other, Garth and I had a personality clash. I had such high expectations of him but he wouldn't fulfil them. One day he would jump a four-foot-square parallel and the next day refuse to go over a trotting pole—that is if you could even get him into the school. So rather reluctantly, especially as he was going perfectly sound, I decided to sell him."

In the meantime, a dedicated young horsewoman named Amy, who already had one of Alan's horses on loan, had been riding Garth. He was not only going beautifully but was indeed perfectly sound. Then, Alan became aware that another curious pattern of events had begun to occur. Every time someone who looked as if he might be a serious potential buyer came to see Garth, the horse would go lame again. His lameness didn't last long, perhaps just a few days.

Puzzled, Alan asked Julie to come and have a look. They watched Garth come out of the box and trot up the yard, indisputably lame on his right front leg. But this time, they both noticed something unusual. In fact, so unusual that Julie hesitated for a second before she remarked on it.

"I looked at Alan, and he looked at me, and I said, 'He went off lame on the right fore and came back on it sound, and now he's lame on the near fore. He's putting it on. He's not lame at all.'"

Julie's assessment was correct. Astonishing, perhaps, but true. Garth had been feigning lameness, something not altogether unknown, according to old horsemen's stories. By this time, Alan was in no mood for games, and utterly exasperated, he saddled Garth up at once and set off on a ride destined to reveal lameness if it was present.

"I took him up to the field and went into canter and gallop. Then I jumped him three times around the cross-country fences, and when I trotted him back to the village, he was steaming but absolutely sound from then on."

Since Garth was now perfectly fit, Alan took him to a local dressage competition. But the horse had other ideas, and they didn't include competing.

"I couldn't believe it! He came out of the box absolutely hopping lame. I turned to him and said, 'Look here, if you can't stay sound, you're not worth anything to anybody. You're too ruddy big to live in a field, you can't be a companion, so you'll just have to go and meet your Maker.'"

Garth was certainly too big and too talented to spend his life mooching about in a field. He was also very expensive to keep fed and shod, to say nothing of the considerable veterinary bills that had already accumulated. A satisfactory outcome to the situation had to be found.

Alan asked Julie to do a further check and see if she could find out what was wrong. What was going on with this curious performance of lameness one day and soundness the next? And most importantly, what did the horse really want? By this time, Alan was in no doubt that Garth was very bright indeed and quite capable of making decisions of his own. The horse made his wishes known to Julie. It appeared that he was definitely not lame.

"He wanted," said Julie, "to go and live with a slim blond-haired girl with a ponytail. Once he's with her, he'll be perfectly sound. He told me that he suffered a kind of loneliness when she went away. He loved the scent of this girl, and he was desperate to make sure they didn't sell him to the wrong person. He didn't know how to tell them what he wanted. He did all he could, as a horse, to make sure they didn't move him away; he limped and hobbled, waiting until someone came along who could understand the pictures he kept sending."

It took everyone—Julie, Alan, and Amy—a little while to realise that the owner Garth had chosen for himself, the slim, blonde girl with a pony-tail, was Amy herself. So Alan sold him to Amy and her family, secure in the knowledge that a mutually compatible partnership between horse and rider had been successfully negotiated.

In hindsight, Alan remarked, "Garth was definitely the most complicated and difficult horse I've ever owned, and easily the most complex."

The highly intelligent and complex Garth succeeded in getting Amy, the owner he wanted, and found himself comfortably installed at the Jerrard family stables. Their rambling, Georgian house holds a diverse mix of children, grandparents, friends, dogs, and cats weaving seamlessly in and out. Laura has kept and bred horses since her early twenties, and Amy trained as a British Horse Society Instructor.

Despite their considerable experience of the equine world, Garth has been something of a revelation for the Jerrards, just as he was for Alan, although Amy admits that it was not immediately love at first sight.

"I first saw him at a dressage competition with Alan. He obviously caught my eye because of his size and presence. When I first rode him, I got on very well with him, but there was still no real connection. After I'd ridden him for a while, it became clear that he liked me. When I was on foot, he used to follow me around the school like a big dog.

"When we learned that Garth had given Julie this picture of a small girl with a long, blonde ponytail and that she was the person he wanted for his owner, we were amazed. We needed to buy another horse for me to compete on, and for Mum and me, that was it! It suddenly all fell into place, and we felt that having Garth was obviously meant to be. When we finally brought him home, he told Julie he had wanted me to buy him because he liked me—he thought I smelled good."

The Jerrards soon discovered other aspects of Garth's lively intelligence.

"He needs constant entertainment," said Amy. "If things are a bit slack, he'll spend his time working out how to undo his stable door—bolts, clips, padlocks, you name it, he can get it undone."

Not only is Garth canny enough to figure out how to open his own stable door, but he is equally adept at opening the others', too, and letting out his companions. His method is to stroll over and bang the kick bolt open on their doors, then smartly pull the upper bolt back with his teeth. These Houdini-like characteristics, not uncommon in many bright and innovative horses, sometimes present a challenge to the Jerrards. Amy is aware that, "If he ever works out his latest bolt, I'm stuck!"

Garth had not long been with the family when, to their surprise, he began showing marked reluctance to load. The reluctance gradually turned to downright refusal to enter the horsebox. Laura and Amy could find no obvious reason, so Julie was asked to see if she could discover the answer.

"It was simple," Julie said, "I asked him why he wouldn't go in the lorry and he told me he didn't like travelling on his own. He wanted a little gelding to keep him company. He was very specific about this, but he was also very polite in his asking, very respectful."

Wanting to make sure that their horses had every reasonable wish granted, Laura and Amy went in search of a suitable travelling companion for Garth, and they found Rupert.

"He's a miniature Shetland and absolutely delightful," said Laura. "Garth thought so too, and from the moment we got him, Garth has never shown the slightest hesitation about going in the lorry. Just occasionally, Rupert will be a bit naughty and Garth will hesitate. But as soon as Rupert pops in, Garth follows."

When Amy first started eventing with him, she was rather nervous about some of the jumps and made a point of asking Garth to take care of her. But although he went round the cross-country course with great enthusiasm, the moment he went into the show jumping ring he would become uneasy and often refuse to finish the course. Unable to find a reason why, Amy asked for Julie's advice.

"Garth told me," said Julie, "that because he was such a big horse, he found jumping in the confined space of a ring quite difficult. Then, he said that Amy had asked him to look after her, so he figured that she didn't like the look of the jumps in the show ring either, so he would simply refuse to do it."

Garth, a talented and remarkable gelding, achieved an exceptional level of communication. It would seem that many more horses, given the opportunity, have views to express.

∞

Perhaps horses choose their owners a great deal more often than even their owners realise. After all, it frequently happens with dogs or kittens. Many people have gone to visit a litter of pups with the intention of coming home with say, the black-and-tan bitch, but have ended up with the all-white dog puppy, simply because he hurled himself onto their lap and refused to move.

It's true that it's probably harder for the horse to get our attention and make his wishes known. Horses being trotted round the auction ring have their work cut out for them. *Excuse me, I don't really fancy that person who's bidding, but I do like the one opposite him, so I'm going over there*, probably doesn't cut much mustard. With a quick tug on the head and a sharp word from a handler, further opportunities for an equine to select an owner disappear faster than soup off a spoon.

Garth had definite ideas of his own. He had some very sensible thoughts about shoes and how he wanted to be shod. He knew when he'd had enough of being in the stable and was pretty adept at letting himself out, and his friends, too. Above all, he was extremely clear about who he'd like for his owner and was prepared to go to some lengths to make sure he got her.

He was not the only one.

Stella

The black mare stood very still amongst the crowds. She appeared to take little notice of pop music belting out of the loudspeakers, babies in buggies, farmers laughing and shouting, and the constant swell of a strolling crowd intent on amusing itself on a sunny afternoon. She had caught sight of someone, and she stared at her as hard as she could. All her attention, every scrap of her energy, was fixed on the woman's face. At last, she was rewarded for her patience and persistence. The woman came closer, unable to ignore the silent summons.

"You're very beautiful," she said, stroking the neck of the black mare. The mare put her nose close to the woman and sniffed delicately. She smelled right. When the saddle was put on her back and the woman mounted, the mare was very careful. She felt sleepy, not as alert as she would normally be and as she trotted off, just a little stiff. But the gash on her hind leg seemed less painful when the woman was near. To the horse, her presence was comfortable and comforting.

"I couldn't resist her," said Annabel, "she was the most striking creature, and she had such presence."

Annabel bought the black horse at a fair and later asked Julie to come and check her over and give her any background information she could. Although the mare had been quiet enough at the start, Annabel discovered she hated having her feet picked up and was rather more nervous than she'd seemed at first.

"This was a lovely mare," said Julie, "who knew right away who she wanted to be with. She'd worked so hard trying to attract Annabel's attention, and she succeeded. She was certainly doped when Annabel saw her at the fair. She said she was given something that made her feel relaxed, but it had no ill effects apart from giving her a 'zonking' headache. It was some sort of herb rolled onto the bit, which tasted very strong and bitter. Her early life was extremely tough, and she had been knocked around the head a good deal, but she knew she would be fine with careful handling. She was very generous natured and quick to learn."

Annabel had decided to call the mare Stella and wanted to know if she liked her name.

"She liked it very much," said Julie. "She'd only ever been called 'stupid' before. They kept saying, 'Come on, stupid.' She thought that was her name."

Whether or not the mare knew the meaning of the word "stupid" is a moot point, but she most certainly responded enthusiastically to the gentle and evocative name of Stella. In Chapter Ten, there are more examples of how important a name can be to a horse. Many of them show a keen awareness of what they are called.

∞

Simba

Veterinarian Josie says, "As a vet, I'd call myself an artist and not a scientist. I'm not fond of gadgets or absolute ways of treating things in black and white. I work in shades of grey and rely heavily on my five senses and another sense I don't understand and want to develop."

She first met Julie at an equine clinic.

"I was watching this Thoroughbred called Simba, an eventing mare, and I noticed that she was behaving in an odd sort of way. She was totally ignoring her rider, which was most unusual because he was the kind of person who was always very much in tune with his horses—they listened to him. But on this occasion, the mare definitely wasn't paying him any attention at all. She seemed much too keen to get to someone else. Again, that was odd, because she was normally rather standoffish. Her ears were directed towards Julie, and every time she circled the school, she kept making a beeline towards her.

"Eventually, the rider gave in and let the mare go over to her. The horse just—well, pushed everyone else out of the way. Then, it became quite obvious that Simba was communicating with Julie. There was no question of it. I just stood there with my mouth open.

"I guess there are people who would have noticed how the mare was behaving and thought, 'Oh well, she's not going forward—just napping, that's all.' But I came with an open mind, and when you used another of your senses and you pieced it all together, it was clear that something unusual was going on."

Simba, the mare who was prepared to disobey her rider if it meant getting Julie's attention, certainly knew what she wanted. Julie herself, not easily surprised by what horses sometimes ask for, was astonished, on this occasion, by the mare's requests.

"I remember," Julie recalled, "that she told me her eyes were bothering her. They were very sensitive to light, and the glare of the white sand in the outdoor school troubled her. Could she have something to go in them that would be soothing? I wondered if some eye drops, would be all right. One of the vets said, 'Yes.' But that wasn't enough for the mare. She really wanted something more, and I got a clear picture of sunglasses. I wasn't quite sure how we were going to arrange that one!"

Josie, meanwhile, had been watching closely, and was astounded by the degree of communication that existed between Julie and the mare.

"I thought," said Josie, "that what the horse wanted was very reasonable. It's just not something that we might have arrived at immediately. The best answer for her eyes seemed to be the kind of shield that police horses wear. I suggested that the owners get one for Simba—and it worked perfectly."

∾

Bobbie

As a former horse professional and lifelong rider, Kate has a wide range of equine experience to draw upon. This was certainly a major source of strength to her when she came to face the challenge of getting a severely injured horse back, not only to health and soundness, but to winning form.

Bobbie is a 16.1 hand, three-quarter Thoroughbred, bay gelding with whom Kate has now forged a very strong partnership, although he was not immediately her dream horse.

"To be honest, although I liked him because he was obviously a good sort and had a big, kind eye, he was a bit too quiet and docile for me. I had him first of all on loan, as his owners wanted him brought on to do a bit of eventing."

But Bobbie, quiet and docile or not, had a strong will of his own, which he was soon ready to demonstrate.

"In the first couple of days, I just couldn't get on his back. In the end, I hopped on bareback, and once we got away from home, he was fine. His owners suggested that I ask Julie to come and see him and find out what was going on. I admit I was pretty sceptical and didn't really know what to expect. Julie found that he got indigestion from sugar beet. As it happened, I'd only put him on it two days earlier, but I'd noticed as I stood in the stable that his stomach that was gurgling away.

"Then we went through his tack. He told Julie the bit he preferred was a straight bar, rubber Pelham, which was useful to know. Very importantly, I learned why he'd been awkward to ride the first few days. Apparently, his saddle didn't fit well, and he wasn't comfortable, so he just didn't much fancy being ridden. Fair enough! We got the saddle sorted, changed his food, and he was fine."

Despite a slowish start, Kate soon found that Bobbie had a lot to offer.

"He was a horse who was happiest doing things. He liked to be occupied."

By now, he'd settled in so well and such a good partnership was beginning to form that Kate decided to buy Bobbie. She continued to spend a lot of time schooling him and doing a few local shows. But in early spring, she moved him to a different livery stable, and the tranquillity of his life was suddenly and sharply disturbed. On the first day in his new establishment, Bobbie was kicked in the field.

"I was told, 'Get over here as soon as possible!' By the time I arrived, the vet had already been called out and I found Bobbie all bandaged up. The next day, when the bandage came off, he had a very bad, three-inch gash on his offside hind leg, just below the hock. For the next few days, Bobbie was poulticed and bandaged on both his back legs, from hoof to thigh.

"About a week later, I got a frantic call from my partner to say that Bobbie was covered in sweat and obviously in a lot of pain. I got there just before the vet. Whenever Bobbie is in pain, he shuts his eyes and shakes his head, and he was doing that like mad. He was obviously very distressed.

"It turned out that the whole leg was infected. For the next ten days,

I had to inject him with antibiotics. The vet came every other day to give him an anti-inflammatory injection.

"We were getting very anxious because his fetlock kept dropping, and there was a possibility that a tendon had been severed. If it had, well, there's usually only one solution for that, and I didn't want to think about it."

With a block of wood strapped under his fetlock joint to give him support and hobbling on three good legs, Bobbie was taken to the university veterinary hospital where he underwent several hours of intensive examination. The conclusion was that the superficial flexor tendon had been completely severed, and the deep digital flexor tendon had been severely traumatised.

The prognosis was not good. The veterinary surgeons thought it was unlikely he would ever be able to event again and possibly might never even be sound. Since it was too long after the accident to operate and put carbon fibre implants in the leg, the choices were limited. Kate could have him put down. Or, she could wait and see what happened.

"We were able to take him home again that night wrapped up in cotton wool. He practically ran into the horsebox to go home. We got him safely back, had his shoes removed, and I phoned Julie for advice."

Julie was deeply impressed by Bobbie's courage.

"He was such a brave horse. He was in an awful lot of pain. I would give him healing for about forty-five minutes each session. After about fifteen minutes, we'd stop and have a break. Then, when he'd had enough, he'd say so. His treatment was defined by him—he just told me what he wanted and I did it."

Kate confirms how clear the horse was about what he needed.

"If anybody had any doubt about healing or Julie's ability, they'd only have to watch Bobbie's response to her treatment. He'd stand for fifteen minutes, almost to the second, with Julie working on his leg. Then he'd lift his leg up and shake it. This would happen two more times, then he'd turn round to her and lay his head on her as if to say, *thank you—that's enough for today.*"

Julie continued to treat Bobbie every month. The healing benefited Kate, too.

"Sometimes, Julie was the only thing that gave me hope as she was the most positive out of everyone. She could tell me how he really was, how he was feeling, and not just how we thought he was."

Two months later, by the end of May, Bobbie was off all medication, including anti-inflammatory injections and painkillers.

"I have a lot of respect for homoeopathic treatment, and ever since the first week of Bobbie's accident, I'd been giving him different remedies. I'd offer them to Bobbie twice each day and he'd choose exactly which one he wanted. It was never the same two days in a row."

Rest was also an important part of Bobbie's recovery programme, but after almost three months of it, he was making it plain to Julie that he wanted to walk on his leg, to move and stretch. Veterinary advice had been to prohibit exercise.

"I've come across a lot of horses who've been put on stable rest," said Julie, "and they always tell me they want more exercise. But obviously, they can't go careering round a field and do themselves still more damage."

"In the end," Kate said, "I compromised by walking him to the end of the yard and back, twice a day. It was only about two hundred yards, but it seemed to add excitement to his life and he certainly seemed much happier after that."

When Kate took Bobbie back to the veterinary hospital for a further check-up they were, as Kate put it, "Absolutely amazed at his progress. When I said I'd been leading him out, the general feeling was that this mustn't be done too soon, as it can cause the scar tissue to stretch, and as a result, cause dipping of the fetlock again. But actually, the gentle exercise he'd done had proved to be a good thing for Bobbie. It had kept the superficial tendon supple and stopped it from fusing and becoming rigid."

In an effort to find a compromise between the exercise the horse considered he needed, and the professional advice to keep movement limited, Kate moved Bobbie to a place where he could have a field to himself, using electric fencing to make him a small, grazing circle about twenty feet across.

"It meant that even though he was still on stable rest, he could be turned out for an hour and feel like a real horse again," Kate said.

Julie continued to come once a month to give Bobbie healing.

"He was very funny," she recalled. "He could tell you just what was going on during the day and he had plenty of comments on the other horses. But now, as he got better, the healing time he wanted grew shorter."

Two years after his accident and a programme that had included the best of orthodox medicine coupled with rest, healing, homoeopathy, and close attention to the horse's own wishes, Bobbie was once again a sound horse.

In mid-summer, Kate took him to a local show where two years earlier, he had won a trophy for ridden hunter.

"We won the trophy for a second time! It was just amazing and wonderful. It was a very emotional day, and a fantastic reward for all that Bobbie had been through, and for everybody who had been involved with getting him fit and well again."

The odds were certainly against Bobbie making such a good recovery. One of the university veterinary specialists, delighted to hear of the final outcome commented, "Owner motivation is a considerable force."

The Old Mare

It was more and more difficult to keep moving. Sometimes, her legs seemed too weak to carry her. But she was wary of lying down in the deep straw, uncertain if she would have the strength to rise again. It took her a long time to eat her food, despite the tender care with which it was brought her. Surrounded by loving concern, nevertheless, the pain grew deeper and a bit more angrily into her belly. Her weariness increased each day, until only a profound longing was left, to journey to the place where there was neither pain nor shadow but only the gentle embrace of infinite light.

There is another matter upon which horses know their own minds and where we can give them a choice, if we're brave enough to do so. It is in choosing life or death. As human beings, we have it in our power to allow a fatally injured or terminally ill animal to die in peace, without further suffering. It is a gift that we can give to animals.

Josie has seen too many examples in her years as a veterinary surgeon and in her work with Julie, to simply ignore what cannot always have immediate scientific validation.

"I'd been keeping an eye on an elderly mare for one of my clients. The little horse was slowly losing weight and getting very stiff. Her quality of life had really deteriorated. I got the feeling that she'd given up, and it was kindest to put her down. But the owner had just gone through a major trauma with a very unhappy relationship. The mare was her prop, and she couldn't cope with the idea of losing her. She was sensible enough to know in her heart it needed to be done but couldn't face it happening. I thought Julie would be able to tune in to what the mare really felt and whether she was ready to go or not."

When Julie arrived at the stables, Josie and the owner were already waiting.

"I asked the mare if she could go on for another six months," Julie recalled. "I knew that it was possible for her to be pumped up with drugs and be kept going. And, I knew how much her owner loved this horse. She meant the world to her. But, I was being asked to find out what the mare really wanted and that's always an awesome responsibility. Not just for me, but for anyone.

"I got a very clear response. She showed me a picture of her stomach, and there was one big lump and some smaller ones. She said she felt tired and wasn't going to get any better. There was absolutely no doubt about what she was conveying. I had the strongest sense of her message: *please let me go.* The feeling that came from this was so strong it almost made me dizzy. I actually stood all of us in line—the horse, her owner, Josie and me, so that I would generate enough energy to allow them to feel what the horse was experiencing. The whole place, at the time, had such a lovely, gentle atmosphere. It seemed that the horse was gently coming out of her body— just light and wonderfully peaceful."

Her owner, moved by such a profound experience and certain now of the horse's wishes, found the courage to have the mare put down there and then.

Josie said, "She was utterly convinced that it was the right thing to do and had no further reservations. She told me it took away her guilt because she realised it was what the horse wanted. I was really glad Julie was able to do so much to help the owner find peace of mind. Otherwise, I knew she would have reproached herself endlessly, wondering if she'd done the right thing."

Not long before, Josie had taken a blood sample from the mare, which pointed towards an abdominal tumour. When she carried out a post-mortem examination, she did indeed find a large tumour. It corresponded with the visual image that the horse had shown to Julie.

There was no doubt about the mare's request to have her life brought to an end. Almost anyone who has ever owned a horse, or any companion animal, has been faced with the dilemma of whether or not a suffering creature should be euthanised and has agonized over the decision to bring its life to a close. Quite apart from the misery that many owners understandably feel, it is arguably the most hated task on the veterinary agenda.

It also raises another point about the kind of choices horses would make, given more of a chance to do so. Remember Garth's story, in Chapter

Four, when Alan became so exasperated with the horse's intermittent lameness that he declared to him, "If you can't be got sound, you'll have to meet your Maker!"

What had Garth made of such a threat? Julie asked the horse himself, several years after he was well established in his new home with Amy.

"It was interesting," said Julie, "because he wasn't fussed about it at all. Death didn't worry him. What bothered him far more was having a saddle that wasn't comfortable or any kind of pull on his mouth—or any piece of tack or equipment that made it hard for him to see where he was going."

In questioning horses about separation in Chapter Three, they certainly were aware of their friends' absence if they simply went on a hack or off in the horsebox to a show or a competition. What appeared important to them was to know *where* their friends had gone.

"Personally," Julie commented, "I've not found that horses are troubled by the idea of death. Most of them have a very matter-of-fact approach and consider that it's where we're all going anyway, so why fret?"

WHAT HORSES SAY

At that time of questioning, all the horses were in very good homes. However, given that horses might wish to make choices if invited to do so, sixty-two horses and ponies were asked:

Anything you'd like to change about your present circumstances?
Sixty-eight percent of the horses were now happy and content with their life. Some of them, who had known really tough times, said they were *more than content.*

Thirty-two percent had a qualifying point to make: almost a third of these wanted some aspect of their lives improved or changed, with most wanting *to be turned out more, with more time in the field and less in the stable.* Several horses responded by asking for *a bigger stable* or wanting *to see more from the stable.* Others in this group replied that they would *like to do more.* They were keen to get out and take part in activities. Perhaps, though, the most touching answer to the question about change came from the dear old mare who said she'd *like to be younger,* a sentiment that could have an echo in many a human heart.

Given a choice, which do you prefer, field or stable?

Seventy-six percent of the group preferred the field. There was no qualification or hesitation about this, no matter what the weather or the circumstances. For the vast majority of the horses questioned, the field was undoubtedly the best place to be.

The remaining twenty-four percent had an interesting and reasonable take on this question. They expressed a liking for both field and stable, depending upon the weather—particularly if it was wet. Several of this group were elderly and felt the cold, but most of these "dissenters," were stallions.

SUMMARISING THE HORSES' VIEWPOINT

Freedom to Choose

There are clearly many equines who can detect which human beings they would find most compatible, and they do their best to gravitate towards them. As well as choosing their owner, some horses seem quite capable of designing their shoes, selecting the right saddle, and requesting suitable companions. When given a choice, they appear to know how often, and for how long, they require healing. In short, there are certainly horses who know their own minds.

The problem is, we often refuse to believe they have a mind. Even when they demonstrate plainly that they do, we're not always willing to comply with their requests.

Year after year, day after day, Julie has been listening to horses and there is still one thing that they desire that we often seem reluctant to grant them.

"It is," said Julie, "the freedom to be a horse. They're willing to do what we ask of them, but when their work is done, they want the freedom to run and roll and play, and simply be a horse. They need to exercise their own nature."

Bearing in mind the number of hours that the modern horse is confined, this seems a fair request. Moreover, if a horse in his natural, undomesticated environment travels up to twenty-five kilometres a day in search of food, it's obvious that being stuck in a stable for much of the time and not getting adequate exercise is a cause of many ills. Garth, of course, simply decided matters for himself by opening his stable door, and then doing the same thing for his companions.

However, the stallions who considered a large comfortable straw-filled stable better than a cold damp field in pouring rain and chilling wind, may be revealing an equal degree of equine intelligence. Or, possibly, they give credence to the old saying that, "With mares you ask, with geldings you tell, but with stallions, you discuss!"

Being pleasantly occupied and able to work is something most horses would choose. It may well be that inactivity is the curse of the modern equine, just as much as overwork was of the nineteenth-century horse.

Julie relates a delightful story of a splendid dressage horse called Buzz who had made it to Prix St. Georges and thoroughly enjoyed his work. She had seen him a number of times and felt there was something, "Not quite right with his back legs. I'd ask him if there was anything wrong, and he'd say, *no*, in a very brusque manner. Either that, or he'd switch off and wouldn't answer me. But, I kept feeling there was something not right there, despite what he told me."

Later, after a flexion test performed by the veterinary surgeon, Jonathan, a bone spavin—a degenerative bone disease—was diagnosed and later confirmed by X-rays. Jonathan wasted no time in teasing Julie that she had failed, "To pick that one up!"

Julie hotfooted it over to see the horse.

"I asked him why on earth he didn't tell me what was wrong! I told him I'd kept on asking him. He just said, *oh, they're making too much fuss about it. It doesn't hurt me very much. If I'd told you, they'd have stopped riding me.*"

"Buzz," his owner says, "has a temper tantrum if the horsebox goes off without him. If the ramp is down in the yard, he'll simply load himself. He loves his work and generally being the centre of attention."

Horses are constantly sending us signals, which, if we are alert to them, can prove richly rewarding for horses and human beings alike. It's up to us to read the signs and see if we can give them greater freedom to make choices that are not only in their best interests—but in ours as well.

CHAPTER 6

The Horse Who Found a Home Forever

6

Kindness, Confidence, and Trust

Liam

Sometimes he shook so much it was almost impossible for him to stand up. It happened at night so only the stars saw him trembling. Fear made him desperate to run, but the hobbles held him tight. He would try to kick away the unseen fear but always the hobbles kept him prisoner. The nights were bad and the days no better. When the people came, the food they gave him tasted sour, like their odour, especially the man with black hair. Small children waved coloured flags in his face. He screwed up his eyes in terror, torn between hatred and despair. Nothing in the world seemed good—nothing, until she came.

"I wanted to find a replacement for a much loved Welsh cob. I knew I needed another horse and I saw this advertisement in *Horse and Hound*, only two lines, no more than that. It said 'Cob, bright bay, good on road, 14.1.'"

Just seven words is not a lot to go on in the search for the perfect horse. But Annie, like Pippa, is a woman who has never lost touch with her intuition. Her nursing training and the difficulties life has strewn in her path have given her warmth, patience and understanding—qualities she extends to people and animals alike.

For more than twenty years, she's taken on rescue animals or difficult horses. At one point, her husband urged her to have a "horseless" year. So instead, Annie adopted six milking goats and ten Jersey cows. Because she enjoys a challenge, she took on a pair of alpacas that she set about training to harness. Alpacas aside, one of the most challenging four-legged creatures in her life has been Liam, a bright bay, Welsh cross cob.

The seven-word advertisement that stirred Annie's intuition into action brought her to Liam's yard. On the basis that two pairs of eyes may be better than one at assessing a horse, Annie took a friend along with her. It was a cool day in midsummer, when horses should be looking their very best, sleek-coated and gleaming.

Not so the one she'd come to see.

"There was this very thin horse," said Annie, "so thin his head looked absolutely huge. His mane was hanging down almost to his knees, his tail was dragging on the ground, and he looked thoroughly unhappy. They offered to tack him up, but he was so head shy they had to take the bridle to bits to get it on."

Nevertheless, they did tack him up eventually and Annie rode him down the lane. Slight and petite though she is, Liam was so weak physically that she soon got off and led him back.

"Oh, and he was very 'bargey.' But, I knew I just had to have him. I felt he wanted to come with me. He seemed to be pulling me towards him all the time. I don't exactly know how to describe this, but he sent off a wave of positive energy to me. It was a bit like the way you click with someone, a person that is. But maybe deeper."

Many people have reported a similar feeling when they first set eyes on a horse with whom they were to develop a deep and enduring bond. Like falling in love, it simply isn't something that can be rationalised.

"My friend said, 'I've no idea how you're going to cope.' I wasn't too sure either, after seeing the performance with the bridle! But, there was an expression in his eyes…I simply knew deep down that I had to have him and he had to come to me."

A four-year-old horse that's thin as a hat rack, head shy, unmannerly, with very little schooling might not immediately rise to the top of a prospective buyer's short list. At this point Annie was, she says, "Slightly sensible." She went away to think about it.

This kind of thinking, to anyone who knows about the experience of finding a horse you can't live without, might be re-titled "playing for time." It simply allows a moment's grace, in which to reassure sceptical-minded friends and relatives. Then, like the truly besotted, the individual must return to the object of his affection, no matter how much head shaking or "tut-tutting" may be going on in the background.

"But, I went back again and fell in love with him even more. I bought him there and then. I knew instinctively that we'd learn together. I just knew it. I made the decision that I was going to keep him forever, no matter how difficult he might be. That was it. He would have a home for life."

By any standards, Liam was a difficult horse. His previous owner, a sometime dealer, had bought Liam at a gypsy auction. When Annie acquired him, although he was almost four years old, she decided he was in such poor condition that further education would have to wait until he was fitter and more stable.

"He was so weak and frightened. We kept finding one problem after another. There were all sorts of behavioural traits that weren't always easy to deal with. He was very unmannerly in the stable, very difficult to catch and when he was walked out in hand, he'd push and pull about. He was still dreadfully head shy, too. And, very worried by small children. He didn't like them anywhere near him. You couldn't even let them stroke him.

"Even out hacking he wasn't easy. He could be really quite tricky. He had a habit of seeing things in the hedgerows. Then he'd have a violent reaction, jumping about and shying sideways. But, he was such a clever horse. I have to say there were days when I wondered if he was pretending, just having me on."

Liam was not pretending. Julie learned later that his super-sensitivity coupled with bad experiences in the past kept him permanently near the edge. He was also having problems with muscle spasms and Annie asked Bill, a veterinary surgeon, to check him over.

"Bill was very good with him because he most certainly wasn't an easy horse to deal with. One vet in Sussex was actually forced over the stable door. Anyway, Bill took a look at him and said, 'You need to get someone to come and see what's going on with this horse,' and he recommended Julie Dicker."

Liam was now almost eight and had been with Annie for four years. There were times, during this period, when the cob had been quite wild. He had developed physically and was now a strong horse and very different from the rake-thin animal Annie had brought home. After some of the duo's more hair-raising moments, Annie's family and friends had become concerned about her safety.

"Every time we had a bad session and somebody would say, 'For goodness sake, why do you put up with that horse? He's dangerous. You should sell him,' something in me just developed even more resolve. I'd say to myself, there has to be a reason for all this. I am not giving in."

"What was immediately obvious about Liam," Julie remembers, "was that he was incredibly anxious. He said that he kept thinking he was afraid but he didn't know what he was afraid of. He was a horse who didn't know how to love human beings. But he was desperate for love himself."

Julie gave him healing and Liam's behaviour steadily improved, although it was several sessions later before he showed her a good deal of information about his past. What he revealed clearly distressed him as much as it did Julie and Annie.

"From the kind of horse he was, I knew it would take a little time for the friendship and trust to build up," Julie said, "but after a couple of visits, things began to come out in the open. Horses don't immediately talk about the bad times to a stranger. Like us, some of them want to block things off and never think of them again. I never, ever push them. That would be fundamentally wrong. Whatever they tell me, good or bad, is their choice.

"On about my third visit, Liam wanted to tell me about his past. He loved Annie and wanted her to know why he sometimes behaved as he did. Then she'd have a deeper level of understanding and could help him even more. This time, Liam showed me how he'd been tied on his near hind leg with a chain that was so heavy it had actually gone into his leg, just like a noose, and caused dreadful sores. The pain was awful and it had made him extremely sensitive around his lower hind legs.

"He'd also been hit a lot with heavy blows on the top of his head and his forelock. Short, sharp blows. Children had hit him and teased him and the man who'd looked after him had just stood by and watched. He was a changeable, moody person, very unpredictable. It had made Liam confused and terrified because he didn't know why he was being punished. I remember that there was a lot of tension, very deep-rooted, behind the tail.

"He showed me a picture of how he'd reared up and fallen onto the top of his bottom. Then, he gave me a lot of images of the man who'd owned him, a very heavy fellow, with dark hair, and oily, filthy clothes. He was very aggressive, very controlling, and he treated horses like machines."

Julie's ability to fill in some of Liam's background helped Annie to understand his behaviour and reassure her that her persistence, kindness, and firm resolve to stick with Liam through thick and thin was paying off.

"When I first saw him," Annie recalled, "when they were first struggling to put a bridle on him, I noticed that he had a scar behind his ears. Quite a long scar. But I didn't know what had caused it.

"It was only when Julie came that I learned that it had happened when he'd reared up at the gypsy auction and fallen over heavily on his back. Then, when Julie told me about the chain, a lot of other things made sense, too—why he hated having his hind legs touched and why he was so frightened of small children. They had teased and tormented him and used to sit on his back while he was chained up and kick him. Oh, and Julie said they would snatch his food away, just as he was about to eat. Poor thing! No wonder he was so wary and frightened and had so many problems. Who could blame him for being difficult?"

Troubled horses often become noticeably more peaceful when they've had a chance to communicate their anxieties. After Julie's visit, more healing, and Annie's continued empathy, Liam again made great improvement.

"Julie told me to watch his eyes over the next year," Annie said, "because they were going to change."

"I've seen a lot of horses' eyes get bigger," said Julie, "as they get more settled and happy in themselves. Sometimes a horse has small, tight eyes because he's so stressed—so frightened— it's almost as if he has to keep his eyes screwed up to protect himself."

"It was absolutely true," Annie said. "There was so much fear in Liam's eyes when I first had him. They were 'piggy' and small. But, they've softened wonderfully. Now they're big, liquid eyes."

For a while, it seemed that harmony and peace had come to Liam's life. But several years later, Annie bought another horse, a Haflinger called Joe, so that friends could ride when they came to stay. Within a few weeks, Liam started to show signs of stress. He was taking chunks out of the wood in his stable and attacking his hay net. He also seemed to have a sore back. Annie asked Julie to come and see him again. Liam, Julie discovered, did not think much of Joe.

"He did things too fast and got on Liam's nerves!" she recalled.

However, once again, the chance to air his feelings seemed to help the cob find a better level of tolerance towards his new stablemate. Healing and a new saddle seemed to sort out his latest difficulties. But a few months later, Annie noticed that Liam had become highly sensitive to sudden movements and noises. He was also having muscle spasms again.

"He looked worried and anxious and I couldn't understand why. It was becoming impossible to ride him past a wood just up here. He'd try and turn round and canter home. Sometimes, I had to get off and lead him. There was nothing else for it. Other days, if he got out of his routine, he wouldn't let himself be caught in the field or even in the stable. Very often, I'd find him staring out of the door in the direction of the woods.

"He was dropping dung a lot, another sign of worry with him, and being very temperamental about his grooming. It was a struggle to get the bit in his mouth again, and as for being shod, well, his performance with the farrier was simply awful. Even with me beside him, he kept pulling back and rearing up."

In short, Liam was showing clear signs of stress and unease but for no obvious reason. Julie was asked to make another visit, to see if she could learn what was upsetting him.

"I remember," Julie recalled, "that Liam said there were people walking about in the woods who were very quiet. Apparently, they had a crossbow and they were poaching or killing the deer. That was the picture he showed me. He could hear the noise of the crossbow and it made him anxious and upset. He thought they were shooting at him."

Liam's fear had a marked affect on his behaviour. Investigations later proved that both the horse and Julie's interpretation were quite correct. Dead deer were discovered, shot by crossbows. The fear caused by the poachers had been quite enough to trigger off old memories of anxiety and send Liam tumbling backwards into his former defensive attitudes.

Liam and Annie shared a close bond and the horse always appeared very aware of any change in her health. Even a relatively short period of disruption in his routine, when Annie was ill for ten days, brought about an alteration in his behaviour and a tendency to revert to his old, unmannerly ways. But, another and more trying period was in store for them both.

One November morning, Annie was riding the Haflinger, Joe. Just as she was leaning forward in the saddle to open a gate, a neighbouring rider was approaching behind her. Joe shied, Annie was caught off balance, and she had a thoroughly bad fall. In fact, the accident put her out of action for over six months, and by the spring of the following year, she was still not back on form.

"I was very tired, and unsteady on my feet. It was as if I wasn't in my body. I just couldn't seem to connect. My body was working away on its own, and I was somewhere else. I asked Julie to do absent healing for me."

During Annie's illness, a curious pattern of similarity began to emerge. At about the same time, Liam began to lose weight and show signs of depression. When Julie visited him again, she found him very uncommunicative. He was, though, distressed by what had happened to Annie. There appeared to have been a good deal of equine chat between Liam and Joe, with Liam, Julie learned, taking the view that his stablemate was boastful and immature, and had no real understanding of the seriousness of Annie's accident.

"I've been aware many times," Julie remarked, "about how horses talk amongst themselves and relay a good deal of information from one to another. As far as I'm concerned, there's definitely some kind of 'field-and-stable telegraph system' operating all the time. I've noticed it particularly amongst certain groups of horses."

However, although Julie picked up what was going on with Liam—his immune system was low, his liver wasn't right, he felt cold and his nervous system was twitchy—and gave him healing, it was a case for veterinary intervention.

If it were possible, Annie dreaded this even more than Liam, who was not noted for his good behaviour with members of the profession. But in the skilful and experienced hands of Paul, the vet, together with buckets of apples, plenty of positive thought and several supportive friends, the blood sample was taken.

"It was a nightmare," said Annie, "but Paul was absolutely marvellous with Liam. He must have spent half an hour, just talking to him and stroking him before he even began to do anything. Even so, he nearly got squashed against the wall. He was incredibly brave. A friend managed to push Liam away. She was brave, too. Liam went up in the air and came down with the needle still in."

It took a further half an hour before the deed was finally done and Paul later remarked that the blood sample had been taken with, "A little barging, jumping, and sweat!" He mentioned that he'd spent a good deal of time, some months earlier, when Liam had needed a tetanus injection, which had involved, "Grooming, bribery, and the odd apple chunk."

"On both occasions," said Paul, "Liam and I parted on respectable terms."

However, the blood test showed the cob to be anaemic, and Paul equated this with a nutritional deficiency or a possible malabsorption problem. The weight loss, he thought, might well have been due to stress. Julie feels that the abuse Liam suffered in his early home changed his whole character.

"Cruelty," she said, "turned him into an ultra cautious, desperately anxious horse."

Without the kind of constant care and routine, to say nothing of empathy, that Annie has extended to Liam, it's unlikely that such an intelligent and complex horse would ever have gained any confidence or trust at all in human beings. Annie believes the balance for Liam is still quite a fragile one.

"I'm sure he'll always be wary, generally speaking, of men—and change. Change can often be quite disturbing for him."

This was dramatically borne out when the family moved house.

"Liam got very uptight when we first came here. I was having a real problem leading him in hand. He was almost unmanageable and very unsettled, but I couldn't understand what was troubling him so I asked Julie to come and see him again."

In their new home, the fields were larger and more open, and Liam was stabled inside a barn, rather than having the traditional outside door. His box stall was spacious, with a low divide, so he could communicate with his new pony companion. He got on well with the pony and there seemed no obvious reason for his difficult behaviour.

"What Julie discovered was so interesting. Apparently, Liam wasn't getting any sleep, any real rest. The roof of the barn is very high, and when the wind was strong it whistled underneath it. Apparently, the noise disturbed him, and kept him on edge all the time. Not something I'd have guessed really, but it made sense.

"Oh, and the size of his box. He felt uneasy in such a big place. His old one was smaller, with a lower roof. He could look out of the door across the fields. I'd forgotten that he wasn't awfully good with wide, open spaces. Of course, once Julie told me all this, I remembered how anxious he used to get when we rode out on the moors. I think he suffers a bit from agoraphobia."

Since Liam was being so difficult to catch and bring in, Julie suggested an alternative method that proved to work very well.

"Her advice was to, 'Just give him his independence. Let him make his own way in.' So I did."

As there were no roads to cross, it was easy enough to open the gates and let Liam make his way in from the field, going straight into the barn. He does this regularly and clearly relishes the chance to trot in of his own accord. His unsettled and anxious behaviour has changed and he's now relaxed and at ease.

But interestingly, Annie reports that his pony companion, Coco, knows that only Liam is granted this privilege.

"It's fascinating to watch. Coco stays in the middle of the field and waits for me to catch him and lead him in. Liam prances on ahead—if there's an audience, he shows off like mad. There's no doubt that a clear hierarchy has been established, with Liam as boss and senior horse. In this role, Liam is definitely the only one who is allowed to come in by himself. I can see it's something he intends to guard quite jealously. That said, Liam took to Coco immediately, and as soon as he arrived here, they instantly groomed each other and there was no kicking or screaming. I think Liam enjoys having a younger horse around. He can show him the ropes!"

The change in Liam's routine had a hugely positive effect.

"I think that we still do some awful things to horses," Annie said. "We don't always give them companionship of their own kind. We lock them up in stables for hours on end. Many people still use punishment as the main way of training. We don't allow them to have their own space, do we? We invade theirs continually, giving them rules all the time, instead of independence and freedom."

Annie has succeeded in forging a deep and trusting relationship with a horse who, in other hands, might not only have continued to receive abuse but probably would have been written off, fit only for the pet food market.

What has she learned through this often demanding and difficult period?

"It's taught me a lot about myself. I have had to become less hurried. I think I was always going about at speed, trying to get things done, but I've just had to slow down. Animals have an enormous amount to teach us. In our modern virtual world, I think we've rather lost sight of our inner self. Animals have it and rely on it and I think they can teach us to find it again, if we're prepared to sit and watch and listen.

"If we want to improve our relationship with our horse, I think we have to try and spend as much time as possible with him. Maybe sometimes just sit in the field and watch—see how other horses behave towards him, how they react to one another. I think when you're with your horse, you have to be patient and let him communicate in his own language. Any learning between you and the horse has to be enjoyable. When you talk to him, you need to listen to his answers."

Liam's often aggressive and awkward ways had their roots deeply buried in fear, anxiety, and a sense of confusion about what was required of him. His problems serve to highlight the "always a reason" philosophy that informs enlightened trainers and horse owners. It puts the onus on us to try and discover the reasons, as Annie patiently did, rather than blame the horse for his apparent misdeeds.

Liam certainly had good cause for his behaviour. Being consistently treated with kindness built up an enormous measure of trust that transformed his life. In Chapter Four, very much the same kind of patient understanding and sympathy existed between Barouche and his "chosen" owner.

WHAT HORSES SAY

The group of sixty-two horses and ponies was asked the question:

What do you need most from us?
Fifty-three percent, a bare majority, considered that what they needed most from us was *food*.

Forty-seven percent had very individual comments to make, and almost every one of these had to do with love in all its many forms:

affection, understanding, praise, kindness, respect, partnership, being stroked, companionship. These were considered more highly than food.

SUMMARISING THE HORSES' VIEWPOINT

Kindness, Confidence, and Trust

The fact that horses rated food as their first requirement seems eminently practical and not at all surprising. After all, most horses spend a great deal of their life stabled and dependent upon people for virtually every meal. To the stabled horse, we are more or less the sole provider of nourishment.

However, forty-seven percent of the group gave answers that covered a wide range of emotional needs, from affection and praise to understanding and respect. The variation in responses highlights, yet again, the individual nature of the horse, and indicates that, all too often, emotional requirements of animals are not sufficiently recognised, or even acknowledged.

Not every owner has the patience, forbearance, and sheer grit of Annie, willing to stick by a difficult horse, no matter what. She was able to fulfil, for Liam, all that the horses themselves considered important. Love, affection, understanding, kindness, and respect were given him, as well as companionship of his own kind, to say nothing of food and shelter. In other less understanding and patient hands, Liam's life would almost certainly have been totally different and probably very brief.

Julie related the story of a pony stallion named Bilbo, who was prepared to undergo drastic change just to have a more companionable life.

"He told me that he was tired of being a stallion. He was often left behind or shut up when the others went off, and he envied the kind of freedom that the geldings enjoyed. So he asked to be castrated. It was surprising, but there was no doubt at all about what he wanted. His owner decided that if that really was his wish, then she would have him gelded. It may seem unusual but he was much happier afterwards."

We might all expect that horses know they need people to give them food. But, interestingly, what emerged from questioning the group of sixty-two, was that many of them considered it not necessarily the most important thing we could give them. Emotional stability, and the right relationship, for some at least, appeared to nourish them even more than hay or oats.

The fate of a horse depends utterly upon who buys, trains, grooms, and rides him. Sometimes, one individual fills all these roles, and sometimes, many individuals are involved in a horse's day-to-day life. But if, as we have seen, horses are capable of making strenuous efforts to find compatible hands, then missing out on the right human partner, or being at the mercy of the wrong one, becomes even more poignant—especially if we are willing to accept that their hunger is not satisfied simply by food alone.

CHAPTER 7

Horses Aren't Designed to Be Ridden

7

Saddles, Seats, and Perfect Balance

Look, this feels as if knives are stuck in my shoulders, my guts are being squeezed, every nerve in my back is being pinched, and you're on top, permanently leaning to one side. Then you say, in a surprised voice, "He's not going forward as he should." Get this saddle off my back, please, before I am tempted to remove it myself. And you, dear sir or madam, along with it!

Jeremy Bentham, a philosopher who extended his views on ethics to the animal kingdom, remarked over two hundred years ago, "The question is not, Can they *reason*, nor Can they *talk*, but, Can they *suffer?*" It seems no less relevant today. It is certainly the question when it comes to the problems the ridden horse encounters on a regular basis. When we found thirty-seven percent of the horses we'd questioned had reservations about the joys and delights of being ridden, it was important to find out why.

We asked them exactly what they found to be most painful, stressful, and irritating. Their answers were very clear. In addition to the horses we questioned directly, a long trawl through the notes that Julie has gathered over the last few years based on more than two thousand horses also highlighted some interesting trends.

From a veterinary viewpoint, equine specialist Josie says, "I reckon sixty percent of the horses I see have back or wither problems caused by the saddle pinching the trapezius muscle and also giving rise to secondary problems in the forelegs. Frankly, I think ninety percent of horses have a badly fitting saddle at some point in their lives, and this is immediately going to cause the horse pain. You've got to be a very talented rider to sit on a horse with a badly fitting saddle and not influence him adversely."

Abe

Sally has worked as a British Horse Society Assistant Instructor for over twenty years, teaching all levels, from novices to keen competition riders.

As a farmer's daughter who's been surrounded by animals since early childhood and ridden all her life, she's in tune with her horses and quick to pick up on any small cues that indicate all is not as it should be. She had been experiencing some problems with Abe, her nine-year-old, bay, Thoroughbred gelding, an ex point-to-pointer and racehorse.

Although initially rather sceptical about the idea of equine communication, Sally had found Julie's earlier assessment of one of her other horses to be extremely accurate, and as she put it, "I felt this lady knew what she was talking about." So a few months after Sally bought Abe, she asked Julie to take a look at his back.

"I knew he'd had a tumble earlier when he was racing and gone 'arse over tit.' His former owners had been honest about it and when the vet had checked him out, he'd said there wasn't a problem. When Julie came to see Abe, he told her that he didn't like racing and he confirmed, through her, what the previous people had told me. He said he'd had a fall. But, he also said he'd banged his head and it had been at the last jump where he'd tipped over. She gave him healing and he was absolutely fine."

Things went on quite smoothly after that visit, but a year or so later, Abe seemed to be having difficulties again.

Sally said, "When we were show jumping he kept refusing, and I couldn't find the reason. So I asked the saddler to come out and check the fitting. We decided the saddle wasn't right, so we tried a different one. The saddler was certain the second one was a good fit. But Abe still kept refusing at certain jumps, particularly the spread fences. I asked Julie to see if she could find out what was going on."

"He told me straight away," said Julie, "it was the saddle that was causing the problem. He said that he'd been refusing in the first saddle because it had pinched him so much. He'd filled out since Sally bought him and it felt like two knives sticking in either side of his withers. The first one was uncomfortable, he said, but the second one was ten times worse."

Sally found this information helpful but rather disconcerting.

"It made perfect sense. The jumps where Abe had been refusing were the spreads. He couldn't stretch out enough because of the way the saddle was digging into him. I felt very badly about this, and rather cross, too, because I'd had faith in the saddler's expertise and it had caused the horse pain and cost me a lot of money."

The problem was sorted out by changing to a saddler who was able to find the right fit for Abe, as well as for Sally.

"I asked Julie to come along and do a final check. I said, 'For goodness sake, tell me if this bloody horse likes *this* saddle!'"

To the relief of both horse and rider, the "bloody horse" did indeed like the saddle.

Dermot

A potential buyer was trying out a horse at a dealer's yard and remarked that the saddle didn't seem to fit the horse properly. "I can't think why," the dealer replied, "that saddle's been absolutely fine on the other six."

True or not, this is a tale which points out that "shape-changing" can often be difficult to detect, especially when a horse has been laid off work, had an injury, changed hands, or simply grown fatter or thinner. There appears to be no such thing as a "saddle for all seasons." Riders too, wax fatter and slimmer, and an alteration in their weight, or a shift in *their* balance, when the saddle is already uncomfortable, can be the last straw for a horse.

Obviously an uncomfortable saddle is not the cause of every subtle change in behaviour, but it's often one of the possibilities to be explored.

Joan and her Irish Draught, Dermot, had a very alarming experience when a saddle hit a sore spot.

"I'd just tacked him up in the yard and I'd got on him, ready to go down to the sand school. I twisted round in the saddle to call out to a friend where I was off to, when Dermot just collapsed. Then, he went off like a bloody rocket! All four feet shot in the air and the next thing I know, I'm flat on my back in the yard. Somehow or other, I managed to roll underneath him when he was in the air. He shot away, leaving me in a crumpled heap.

"He roared back into the field—all his tack still on, of course, jumping two big gates in the process. I had no idea what could have upset him so much, but it was very worrying. I got hold of Julie and asked her to come and see what was the matter with him."

"He'd taken off," said Julie, "because he knew he'd hurt Joan, and he was frightened. He said that the saddle pinched him. As Joan had twisted around, it had caught a nerve in his withers and he dropped to the floor. He said he just couldn't help himself.

"Joan was determined to find out what saddle he wanted and we must have gone through about seven or eight. We kept plonking them on his back till we got to the last one and he said that was the one that had caused him the bother."

A new saddle was immediately ordered. Not surprisingly, though, Dermot became very touchy about being tacked up after this episode.

"He'd have minor panic attacks when the girth was first tightened," said Joan. "We found the best way to do it was to put the saddle on, and do the girth up very slowly. We'd leave Dermot by himself to walk around the stable for a few minutes before the bridle went on and he was brought into the yard. Usually, he needed to be walked up and down a little longer before anyone got on.

"We realised that Dermot was far calmer when his dressage saddle was used, rather than his general purpose one. The main difference seemed to be that the dressage saddle had a very wide, elastic girth and the general purpose one had a narrower, fabric girth. So an extra wide elastic girth was made to measure for him and now he's absolutely fine to tack up with both saddles."

Will and Jack

Sandy, a horse keeper of many years standing had a request, through Julie, from her Dales pony, Will. Like Sally, she too was ready to do whatever was needed to make her horse more comfortable.

"Will told Julie he wanted a new saddle as the old one was pinching him across the withers and restricting his movement. I duly went out and bought him a new one that was wider, with a straighter cut to allow freer shoulder movement. He obviously knew what he wanted because he did much better in ridden classes this year."

Pippa, introduced in Chapter Three, had also been made very aware of a horse's attitude towards saddles, and when she acquired a new horse, Jack, she asked Julie to come and check him out.

"I'd fitted Jack with a saddle that seemed to me to be okay. I put one or two on him and he pulled faces, so I kept trying until I found one I sensed he was happy with. When Julie came, she told me that the saddle I'd given him was just fine. That gave my confidence a real boost. Jack told her that in the past his saddle had been too tight and it used to cause his right shoulder to jam."

Pippa considers that riders, particularly ones who are new to horses, are often not aware of the needs of the horse.

"I think far too many people are pressured into buying saddles that simply don't fit the horse properly, and the damage that can be done through this is enormous. If we're sensitive to them, horses can make it plain that something is not right. I think a lot of people don't, or won't, open themselves to the way in which horses can communicate with us."

Nigel – Master Saddler

Given the very real nature of the problems that most horses encounter at some point in their lives, despite kind, experienced and sensitive owners, it's easy to see why master saddler Nigel, remarked, "Horses are not designed to be ridden." A closer examination of the anatomical structure of a horse's back makes this plain. The weight-bearing area is remarkably small. Only the distance between the eighth and eighteenth rib on a horse's back can tolerate a rider with any degree of comfort.

Considering that we have been on their backs, literally and metaphorically, for at least three to four thousand years, it's remarkable how slowly the saddle has evolved. The first riders went bareback, then, the Greeks used a horsecloth, which the Romans modified into a rudimentary saddle with rolls and ridges to give the rider some grip.

Little is known after the Roman period, until we reach the early Middle Ages, when, in the eleventh century, a saddle appeared that had the fundamentals of a pommel and cantle.

Our forbears seemed to be aware—for which, long ago, horses must have heaved a sigh of relief—that it was essential to keep pressure off the sensitive equine spine.

"It wasn't until I began to design and make saddles that I remembered the ones I'd ridden in as a child," said Nigel. "I was horrified. I realised immediately how impossible they must have been for the horses.

There was one saddle that was so bad it made my seat bones hurt. I'd end up putting more weight on one side than the other—but I didn't think about the horse or the effect that might have on it. It's only with hindsight, of course, that I've realised what I had been doing to the horse just to help my own problem."

Nigel heartily agrees with the veterinary surgeon, Josie's assessment that ninety percent of horses have a badly fitting saddle at some stage in their lives. But what makes this such a common problem?

"Lack of money and ignorance are enemies of good saddle fitting. Oh, and a certain group of people who know they've got a saddle that doesn't fit, but just won't do anything about it. When I began making custom-made saddles, I became even more aware of how rapidly horses can change shape—not simply from season to season, as you might expect, but even from week to week. Horses are forever changing, but saddles don't change with them. The wrong saddle can be a major source of suffering to a horse, and it isn't put on the horse for just one ride. It's something that happens regularly, so the effect can be cumulative. I say to people sometimes, "Look, consider how you'd feel if you were asked to go for a twenty-mile hike in a pair of shoes that were a size too small.

"It's a very good thing that saddles have changed quite radically in the last ten years. People's minds have become more open, too. Nowadays, most saddlers are happy to work with vets and physiotherapists. Twenty years ago, such a suggestion would have been laughed at. In my own business, I try every single day to improve saddle fitting to give the horse more freedom."

The ideal way to fit a saddle, in Nigel's view, is not in professional isolation but through a team of experts working together.

"Each individual brings his own expertise to the problem and our chances of sorting it out there and then are very much better than when we're all working in isolation. If we trust each other, we can question one another without anyone feeling offended.

"If I'm fitting a saddle when a veterinary surgeon, a horse physiother-apist, and an animal intuitive with the accuracy and integrity of Julie Dicker, are all present, then I consider that between the four of us we can do a really good job for the horse and for the rider. That, for me, is the most rewarding way to do it.

"Certainly there are a lot of ill-fitting saddles out there. There are also a lot of unbalanced riders and quite a few inexperienced owners who are doing too much, too soon. Horse and rider are a team and they must work comfortably together. Of course, there are strong riders who can make a horse go forward, even if he's not comfortable. They know how to make him submit, which isn't good either."

Is there such a thing as a perfectly fitting saddle? Or, is it an anatom-ical impossibility for both horse and rider?

"The best way to fit a saddle to a horse is not to put one on his back. That said, riding bareback can sometimes cause greater pressure than a saddle. What I do is essentially a damage-limitation exercise. I try my best to prevent damage to your horse. Maybe I see three horses a year where you really can't put a saddle on their backs because of their confirmation. Nothing you do will make it fit well enough. So, there is no such thing as a perfect fitting saddle.

"I often get the impression that a lot of people don't really under-stand how costly it is to own a horse. I remember one client, some time ago now, who really needed a new saddle. She was broke at the time and she said to me, 'Look, I don't know who's going to eat—me or the horse.' 'In that case,' I told her, 'Eat the horse!' Quite honestly, if someone can't afford to keep a horse properly, it's better to sell him to someone who can. You've got to have enough money to have him shod regularly and call out the vet whenever it's necessary. It's the same with saddlery. You're putting money to a good cause when you have the right saddle. They all need checking once or twice a year—more often than that, if you suspect a problem. After all, a horse is an athlete and he needs attention if he's to perform at his best.

"Sometimes, when I see a horse that's in trouble from a badly fitting saddle, I think when it's the horse owners themselves who have caused the damage, they're so hurt and distressed by it that they want to pass the buck. They simply can't bear to think of what they might have done, either through ignorance or bad riding. If you're not happy about the way a saddle's been fitted, you've got to question any advice you're given.

"From what I see as a saddler," Nigel continued, "a lot of owners expect too much of their horse. Horses are individuals and have to be treated as such. I wonder how many horse owners really consider if the horse they've chosen is right for what they want to do? Some people love football, others like long distance running or tennis or swimming. They all have slightly different talents. It's the same with horses. Some love dressage, some enjoy endurance riding, some jumping. But, they don't all like the same things.

"Riders really need to question themselves and see what they want and what the horse wants, and find out if they're compatible. If they're not, both of them are going to suffer. We should have reached a stage now where horses can have freedom from pain and freedom from mental cruelty. To see a horse shaking with fear is a terrible sight. I try not to think about how some people mistreat them. It's arrogance that stops us from communicating better with horses. Every time. Impatience, too, because it takes time to bond with a horse. Maybe six months, maybe a year. You'll never stop learning, especially if you listen to them and watch them. Just sit out in the field and build up a bond with them. They'll give you so much and give it willingly. But, that bond of trust and understanding has to be there. We shouldn't take riding horses for granted—it's a privilege, not a right."

WHAT HORSES SAY

Given the horse's power and speed and indeed his intelligence, why on earth should this good animal allow us to ride him at all? There's no doubt that as far as a test of sheer strength goes, the horse is always going to win. Yet even after the rotten treatment horses like Liam or Lucy or Barouche endured in their early years, they still let us ride them. It's not surprising that sometimes they rebel—the wonder is that they don't do it a lot more often.

To learn more, the horses and ponies in our group who were regularly ridden were asked the questions:

Why do you agree to let us ride you?
There were forty-three answers that could be evenly listed under three different attitudes: enjoyment, acceptance, and dislike:

Enjoyment
Sixty-three percent were in favour of being ridden. The pleasure of getting out and about, of seeing new things and *fun,* seemed to be the main theme of this group. It is enjoyable, especially for the more curious animals. *Enjoy it—gets you out* seems particularly important for stallions who, perhaps more than mares and geldings, spend a good deal of time in stables or confined quarters. One horse, a stallion, especially likes *the connection between human and wants to please and give pleasure.* To be ridden makes life *interesting* and clearly the stimulation of new sights is important to the horses' well being. The response to this question correlates with the answer given in Chapter Four when the horses were asked what they enjoyed most in life, and the majority responded *being busy.*

Acceptance
Nineteen percent, however, were not very enthusiastic about the whole

business of being ridden. Acceptance is the key attitude taken by these horses: *because you have to.* One horse actively *wanted to conform—to be told what to do.* But, that was, perhaps, unusual. The rest of them considered: *it's the done thing; what everyone else does; just accept it; don't mind it—it's okay; because you have to, easier to conform.* A couple responded that they like it *sometimes,* but at best it could only be said to be *okay.* Others reported: *like it sometimes; don't like it, but okay.* There is no real antagonism from these horses—more a weary resignation that being ridden was something that was a part of life and it had to be done, whether they liked it or not.

Dislike

Eighteen percent of the horses questioned fell into this category: *don't enjoy it—it's something that just happens,* was a typical response. This seems a great pity, as unlike the group who felt resignation, their attitude was tinged with sadness and sometimes, it seemed, with pain. It was, *uncomfortable now,* for several horses.

Although sixty-three percent found good reasons for being ridden, it is not quite such a large majority as one might hope for, bearing in mind that every one of these horses was in a good home and loved, cared for, or ridden by experienced individuals. Finding that thirty-seven percent were just resigned to the whole business of being ridden, or simply disliked it, is disappointing and, perhaps, rather worrying. However, there were good reasons why some horses showed a real lack of enthusiasm, as we shall see.

What do you dislike about being ridden?

Despite the fact that most of the horses were happy to be ridden, ninety-three percent of the group had some physical pain and irritation. When questioned specifically, it was found that most problems fell into two areas. Not surprisingly, they are saddles and riders!

Physical Pain

For nearly all the horses, saddle problems, ranging from downright ago-
nising to uncomfortable, were a prime source of pain and discomfort: *too
tight; pinches; hurts withers; hurts shoulders;* and the girth was often *too tight*
or *pulled too hard.*

Discomfort caused by the rider's lack of balance or style of riding was
also regarded by the horses as physical pain. Complaints included: *wob-
bled about too much; lopsided; sits too much to the right; sits heavily on the
left.* And, just as uncomfortable were: *sits too far forward; sits too far back;
doesn't sit still; wriggles around too much; legs flap and hit sides; pulls in the
mouth. Rider too heavy* and *rider getting on* were also major problems for
several horses.

Other horses had their own particular physical shortcomings or old
injuries that played up and became aggravated by being ridden: *right knee
hurts; not able to move shoulder; hip problem; can't go so fast anymore; back
hurts behind saddle; back not strong enough and gets sore; feeling stiff; aches
when made to do a lot; hurts going downhill.* A few complained that their
bit was *too cold,* which may well have been because they had particularly
sensitive teeth.

Irritation

Their most frequent complaint was about poor communication—riders
failing to give clear and understandable instructions. Horses were *pulled one
way but asked to go another,* and they often didn't know *which direction they
were going in.* They were given *wrong instructions* and *shouted at.* Generally
speaking, they wanted riders to *slow down* and *be clearer.*

Riders who generally *talk too much* and are constantly *talking to
other riders* were considered irritating, and one horse reported that his
rider's habit of *scratching her face and her specs falling down* was particularly annoying.

One horse, rather endearingly, found it very trying that he was never *allowed to look over the hedge*. Others complained that they weren't allowed to *go fast enough* or had to *come back too soon*. Some disliked *leaving the others* or found it irritating when their *mane was pulled*. *Not getting own way* and *going into outline the way he wants* were also found annoying.

SUMMARISING THE HORSES' VIEWPOINT

Saddles, Seats, and Perfect Balance

Although all this might sound like a woeful catalogue of complaints and clearly, in the words of our teachers' report cards, some horse keepers *could do better*, something very significant and cheering emerges. Horses are forgiving creatures, and on the whole, take a kindly view of us. If they know they're well and truly loved, despite our lapses, they are still willing to be in partnership with us.

Horses are long suffering, and as Julie points out, "Very polite, most of the time." But undoubtedly many riders, even those with the best of intentions and the kindest of hearts, often make their horses' lives more difficult. The most frequent complaint about riders could be summarised by saying that we are poor communicators.

"Over the years," said Julie, "I've found horses have asked again and again for us to be more direct and clear in our communication with them and to take more time. When we're thinking one direction, then pull on the reins asking them to go in the opposite one, it causes them awful confusion. Using different words for the same thing—that makes a problem for them, too. One person says, 'Whoa,' another says, 'Halt,' and yet another says, 'Stop.' It's much easier for the horse if we decide on a word and stick to it."

Apart from our inability to be clear and precise, our manner of riding can often be a source of considerable discomfort. What may seem to us a very slight list to right or left can make a vast difference to the horse. An undetected tendency to sit more heavily on one side than the other, shift around, or flap our legs about can cause horses real misery. Riding in what might generally be termed an "unbalanced fashion" scored high on our group's list of complaints.

Overweight riders, and those who sat down too heavily in the saddle, also got a mention. If the rider was both overweight and sat down like a sack of potatoes, the poor horse's misery was doubled.

A close look through Julie's records of assessments of over two thousand horses in recent years, revealed similar trends to the forty-three horses questioned. Both unbalanced riders and saddle problems occurred with great frequency, with over a third of the horses complaining of uncomfortable or badly fitting saddles and nearly forty percent suffering back troubles.

Equine vet Josie commented, "There's an old horseman's rule of thumb, which I think is very apt. If your weight exceeds a sixth of the horse's body weight, you're affecting the way that horse goes. It can carry a sixth of its weight quite easily, and if you flop around you won't affect him too much. But more than a sixth, you're almost certainly going to be giving the horse a bad time."

Julie has observed many signs indicating potential problems.

"As soon as some horses catch sight of the saddle," she commented, "they cringe or they circle and shift around. I've seen them sink down or try and slide away. Oh, and there's ears back, teeth forward, standing up on two legs. It's a long list!"

All or any of the above can reasonably be interpreted as *for Heaven's sake, let me get the hell out of here* mode. Even if the saddle is fine, the girth can still make a horse miserable. Certainly some girths are appreciated much more than others.

"The preferred type," said Julie, "is the soft, elasticated leather, with a sheepskin covering. That's what a lot of them tell me they find most comfortable."

Even small points, like occasionally being allowed to look over the hedge or snatch an illicit branch from a hedgerow, might contribute greatly to a horse's pleasure in being ridden.

"Horses," said Julie, "definitely need to have the chance to stop and look. Sometimes, it's just plain curiosity, which is fine. Sometimes, it's because they're scared and want to work out what's going on. It's much better for them if we let them assess something—a sound, an unusual object—in their own way, rather than nervously or angrily trying to push them on. They're much more sensitive than us and we need to respect that."

One of the common beliefs that link Julie and her horse-owning clients is the philosophy that for virtually all apparent equine misbehaviour, "There's always a reason." As one breeder remarked, "Almost every difficulty with a horse is to do with pain or fear, either the memory of it or anticipation of it."

That's something every horse owner knows, but clearly, it's one we all too often forget. In fact, many of the points in this chapter are obvious to any experienced horse owner, but they evidently occur more often than might be supposed. Certainly, our equine partners have keen powers of observation, and it seems that little escapes their notice, even some of our smaller mannerisms. If horses don't always enjoy being ridden or simply put up with it in a stoic fashion, we appear to have only ourselves to blame.

Josie succinctly summed up the case for the horses.

"Their biggest problem," she remarked, "is us!"

Foot Notes and Teething Troubles

8 Avoiding Unnecessary Suffering

A wise old mare was giving advice to her offspring, and she said, "Whatever you do, youngster, remember to keep your feet clear, free, and ready to run. If you can't run, then use them to kick away danger. Never let them be caught—your feet are your fortune."

"No foot, no horse" is one of the most familiar sayings in the horse world. But, the actual practice of shoeing, according to some sources, wasn't widespread until well into the eighth century. Its origin is uncertain, but it seems likely the idea was stimulated by a need to protect the hoof from excessive wear when travelling on hard going or in very wet weather, especially in parts of Northern Europe.

But shod or unshod, and whatever level of comfort (or, sometimes discomfort) the horse might experience through wearing shoes, Julie's work has highlighted some of the difficulties that horses can experience during the process of shoeing.

The Brown Mare

One 16.2 hand, Thoroughbred mare of horse vet Josie's acquaintance, definitely fell into the group of horses whose curriculum vitae would not include those magic words, "Good to shoe.""This mare was about six or seven," explained Josie. "She hated being shod. I knew she used to be okay and had never been a problem to shoe when she'd been at livery. But, obviously something had happened somewhere along the line to make her so nervous. The farrier couldn't get anywhere with her and the owner asked me to come over and sedate her. That was difficult enough because the mare wasn't too keen on the whole business."

Josie managed to do the deed. However, an unfortunate pattern was starting to build up because the next time the mare needed a new set of shoes, Josie received another invitation to bring herself and her syringes to the yard.

Since a horse's memory is on a par with the fabled elephant's, or possibly even surpasses it—especially where pain, distress, or injury are concerned—the brown mare remembered Josie rather too well. Unfortunately, the hand that bears the needle is not always equated with the hand that heals.

"Of course, this time it was even more difficult because the mare knew exactly what was going to happen and she wasn't willing to cooperate. The owner wasn't terribly keen to get involved, either! It was virtually impossible to get near the mare. Eventually, we managed, but we had to give her a lot more sedative than the previous time. I wasn't very happy about it all. When the farrier appeared, I could see from the mare's reaction that she was scared of him. He wasn't overly sympathetic to her, either."

On the third occasion Josie received an invitation to the shoeing, she decided to rethink the whole situation. Like all vets, she was well aware of the times when tranquilizing shots are effective and appropriate, but she was also aware of the other occasions when they're merely treating the symptoms and not getting anywhere near the cause. Whatever lay behind the mare's reluctance to be shod, to pump more sedatives into her didn't equate with Josie's professional integrity. She decided there must be another route.

"I suggested to the owner that we get Julie to come and give the mare some healing. I knew the farrier was due at lunchtime, and we reckoned we needed about two hours before he got there to get the mare in a relaxed state."

Julie arrived and sized up the situation. She remembers it very well.

"Josie had already arrived when I reached the yard. I went over to the stable and with just one look at this mare could see she was on a knife's edge. Given half a chance, she'd be really dangerous. Her eyes were out on stalks and she was getting all lined up to give you both barrels."

This time the owner decided discretion was the better part of valour and remained outside the stable. Julie, too, was well aware of the hazards posed by a big, terrified mare who was prepared to defend herself with teeth and hooves against any threat, real or imaginary.

"I knew that the very first thing I had to do," Julie said, "was get absolutely calm. I couldn't do the work I needed to do if I was in any kind of nervous state. I took a few minutes to meditate quietly and just get myself together. Believe me, if I hadn't got so much confidence in Josie, I would have been out of there in a flash!"

Julie usually travels with a small bottle of lavender oil in her pocket. One of the most useful of all essential oils, many horses have a fondness for its calming scent.

"I put some lavender on my wrists and neck. I didn't want even the slightest whiff of fear around me. I knew that would seriously tip the balance in the wrong direction. When I went in the box with Josie, we were very calm, very quiet. Both of us were talking away to the mare all the time. We didn't want to make her feel threatened or any more nervous than she was already.

"She flipped her backside round in full defensive position. Josie got her by the headcollar. There was no doubt she was in a mood to kick you right out of the box. She reminded me of a rocking horse because she'd rock forward and then go backwards ten paces. I was thinking that if she reversed back against the wall, at least she wouldn't be able to kick me. I totally trusted Josie, otherwise I wouldn't have stood there at all. We'd already agreed that if the situation got really bad and the mare wanted to go for either of us, we'd leave her alone. We weren't going to go in and dominate her. She had to be willing to cooperate.

"There was no way you could take any kind of veterinary kit in there," Julie continued, "but I'd given Josie the lavender oil before we went in. She rubbed some on the mare's nostrils and I stood at her neck where she was comfortable with me. I ran my hands over her withers and back. At this point, she started to relax but still had a worried look on her face. She was saying that she wanted me to help, but it was incredibly painful. Her back had been wrong for some time, and she couldn't bear to lift her legs up for the farrier, it hurt so much.

"So I stayed where she was comfortable and used my hands, and even-tually, she settled down. I got my hands in line with her pelvis and she dropped her head. Then, she straddled her hind legs and went into a rocking motion, at which point Josie and I looked at each other, gave a huge sigh of relief and said, 'We've hit the spot.'"

By this time, the back had started to realign itself and the whole atmos-phere inside that stable had changed. The mare was completely quiet, calm, and relaxed.

"We'd been able to get her back sorted, but we wanted to make sure she stayed relaxed when the farrier asked her to hold her legs up," said Josie. "The mare had told Julie that the apprentice was a lot more sympathetic than the farrier, and she wanted the younger fellow to shoe her.

"I wasn't sure we could fix that, so I asked Julie to find out what else the mare wanted to help her when the farrier came. She asked for two doses of Aconite 30C every ten minutes, with five to ten drops of Rescue Remedy, starting about an hour before the farrier arrived. So she had four doses of Aconite and Rescue Remedy on an apple, and she wanted some more oil of lavender rubbed on her nostrils. By this time we could run our hands all over her. She wasn't fidgeting and she told Julie her back was comfortable."

The farrier arrived, dead on time, exactly two hours after Josie and Julie had begun their work.

"He called out, 'Is she doped, then?' and I poked my head over the stable door. I still had the syringe in my pocket. I told him she was ready and she'd be okay now. He said, 'Well, I'm bloody well not going in there if she's not doped.' He sent his apprentice in to take off her shoes. When he went to put the new ones on, the mare was as good as gold. She didn't flinch once. After he'd finished he said, 'There you are! See, it pays to dope them in the first place.'

"I don't blame them for wanting a horse sedated," Josie continued. "It usually does the trick. Quite a lot of horses are awkward to shoe. A very few are genuinely naughty, but most of them are either afraid or in pain. From the farrier's point of view, it's very unpleasant getting kicked or having a fight with a horse. Ordinarily, you might give a tranquilizing shot for the first time a horse was difficult, and then reduce the dose considerably the next time. And hopefully, give the owner some instruction on overcoming the problem, so there's no need to sedate.

"Personally, I find it much more satisfying to work with Julie and avoid the use of dope altogether. That said, I take my hat off to farriers who work extremely hard, often in difficult situations."

∞

Although having shoes put on may seem a relatively uneventful procedure from the human viewpoint, from the horse's it might be seen quite differently. As flight animals relying upon their feet to take them out of danger, their genes still carry the primitive fear that having their feet caught up is a hazardous business. Youngsters who've been accustomed to having their feet picked up and picked out from an early age, and who are used to be being tied up or standing still, generally tolerate the first assault of metal, fire, and clenches well enough.

But the angle and height at which the horse must hold his legs, particularly the hind legs, can make keeping his balance difficult. Standing on three legs isn't natural for a horse, especially if you already have a back problem, like the brown mare Julie and Josie had to deal with. In human terms, it might be a bit like being required to stand on one leg with your eyes shut tight, for at least ten or fifteen very long minutes. If, on top of this, you were also suffering the misery of lower back pain, it's not difficult to see why some horses react as they do.

Hal

Hal was a horse who found having a set of shoes put on very trying. A 17.2 hand Cleveland Bay, at livery with professional horsewoman, Jenny, he's testimony to some of the common difficulties that horses can experience when they're being shod.

Jenny explained, "Hal came over from Ireland as a four-year-old, and we didn't know a lot about him, except that he was bought as a known 'shiverer.'"

Shivering is a condition generally associated with the nervous system. Horses with this complaint tend to have contractions of certain muscle groups, most often in the hindquarters and tail.

"It didn't affect him when he was being ridden but happened more when he'd been standing for a long time. Of course, it made him very difficult to shoe and the first time he was shod here it took a massive dose of sedation and about three people nearly four hours to get the back shoes on. I asked Julie to come and see if she could help him. We also decided to change to a new farrier, and luckily, they both were able to get here on the same day."

"What Hal needed was very simple," said Julie. "He turned round to me and said, *I want to lean against the wall.* He felt that whenever he was being shod and asked to stand on three legs, he would lose his balance and fall over. But, if he could lean against the wall, he was sure he'd be all right. So I said to the farrier, 'Let's try leaning him against the wall.' We pushed his rear end over and he was absolutely fine."

"It totally changed his attitude towards shoeing," said Jenny. "He was happy with the new farrier so there was no need to have a whole crew of us on duty when he was being shod. Then, we found that the previous farrier had got in such a state with the horse that he had more or less 'chucked' the shoes on Hal's back feet. After an X ray, we saw his feet were out of alignment and unbalanced due to bad shoeing.

"We got the angle of his shoes corrected, but maybe a little too suddenly, so he went lame for a while, which affected his shoulder and caused stiffness. Julie came and gave Hal a long session of healing on his shoulder. He came sound again."

Spark

Jane has been a professional dealer for many years, backing and schooling young horses as well as taking on "problem" or difficult horses that need reschooling before they're able to perform at their best. Julie is a regular visitor to the family yard and has helped many of their horses over the years.

"We had a horse here one season," said Jane, "a big, grey, Thoroughbred gelding called Spark. Although he was only seven, and hadn't done a lot, he kept going lame."

Intermittent lameness is one of the bugbears of the veterinary profession; even when using sophisticated equipment, the causes can be extremely difficult to pinpoint.

"We sent him back to his owners for further veterinary treatment. He was diagnosed as having laminitis, and if he couldn't be got sound, it looked as if he might have to be put down. So we asked Julie to come and see him.

"She discovered that he'd been incorrectly shod and had very sensitive feet. We had a good farrier check him out again. He put leather pads under his shoes. Julie gave his back and legs healing, and he was soon able to go on normal food again. One way and another, we got him completely sound, and he went on to a very good new home."

Julie spends her days listening to things from the horse's point of view. Many of the horses' requests are not only reasonable but later prove to be verified by other professionals, as Cedric's story illustrates.

Cedric

Sandy has kept horses for pleasure and showing for many years. One of her equine family, a splendid, skewbald cob called Cedric, who Sandy always referred to as a "wise, old sage," had a specific request about the way he wanted to be shod.

"He'd decided," said Julie, "that he was lopsided and he wanted wedges on his shoes. He was very specific. First of all, Cedric showed me a picture of his foot and then a picture of what he wanted—a slice of something underneath his shoe. It looked a bit like cork. I then sent him a picture of how deep—I imagined he'd want about half an inch. He sent back the picture half the height, and I could see it was probably a quarter of an inch. He then showed me his other hind leg, with the wedge cut in half again, so I guessed that he wanted an eighth of an inch on the second shoe. He showed me quite plainly that he wanted the wedge just at the back of his shoes. It turned out that he wanted a quarter of an inch on the left hind and an eighth of an inch on the right. He was very precise!"

At the farrier's next visit, he agreed that older horses often needed wedges on their shoes and, in fact, put the pads exactly as Cedric had wanted. He was mildly amused to learn later that the request had come directly from the horse. Like Garth in Chapter Five, Cedric had a mind of his own and was quite capable of using it sensibly to improve his level of comfort and well being. All he needed was an interpreter.

∞

Our long-suffering, domesticated horses have become used to shoeing, but deep down, it's still against their basic instincts, a point that is easily forgotten when we become irritated or impatient with a horse that's reluctant to be shod. Of course, since smell, for nearly all horses, is the keenest indicator of what's going on around them, not every equine relishes the odour of burning hoof as hot metal hits horn, painless though it might be. Fire is as frightening to horses as it is to humans, and the smell of anything burning can be sure to raise the equine blood pressure.

As if all this isn't enough, there's the matter of attaching the shoe to the foot with small metal nails, or clenches. When these are hammered in, some horses find it disagreeable. The hammering sets up a vibration in their head and teeth, according to some of the equines that have been questioned on this matter. It might be compared to the effect that we experience when our dentist applies his drill to our teeth. Some of us can stand it and go to sleep while it's being done, and others want to claw their way out of the chair, even with a pain-killing injection.

So it is with horses, too. Unfortunately, there's a usually a human being standing in the way when they wish to express their feelings. Neither farriers, owners, or on the whole, even veterinary surgeons, are terribly keen to be the recipients of the equine equivalent of "Let me get the hell out of here!"

Kate, the owner of Bobbie who was introduced in Chapter Five, has ridden since she was six years old and has spent part of her life working professionally with horses in stud farms, as well as doing a two-year stint as a trainee farrier.

"It's a tough job, and owners expect you to do it well, even with a horse that's had very little handling. It makes a big difference if you go to a place where the horses are well mannered, their feet are clean, and you're given a dry, level place to do the shoeing. Oh, and a cup of tea never goes amiss!"

Several years ago, Kate gave up professional horse work but remains a dedicated horse keeper.

"Speaking now as a horse owner, though, I think farriers are often a bit too impatient, maybe because they're not always given as much time as they really need. Quite a few certainly have a tendency to lift the horses' legs too high. That can be frightening as well as pretty uncomfortable."

Farriers do one of the toughest jobs in the horse world. They come out in all weathers to all kinds of establishments, some good and some not. Their work requires considerable knowledge of equine anatomy and behaviour, as well as strength and patience, with the latter often having to be extended to owners as much as to horses. Moreover, they're expected to be able to deal with every sort of equine, from shaggy ponies to glossy Thoroughbreds. If a set of shoes is required, their task is to get the shoes fitted, no matter how reluctant the horse. However, since most are self-employed, being injured and out of work is definitely not a desirable option.

∞

If your teeth were aching, your gums were sore, and a cold, heavy chunk of metal was jammed between your jaws, would you really fancy doing an hour or two of dressage? Just to add to your misery your rider, who is a tad overweight, thumps down in the saddle and gives you a sharp yank in the mouth. When you get back to the stable, tired, thirsty and decidedly grumpy, the water in your bucket is so icy it makes your already quivering teeth throb with pain. It might be rather tempting to place those unhappy teeth squarely on a tender part of the human anatomy!

This is not an exaggerated picture of how a horse might feel. A careful look through Julie's records over recent years revealed that close to seven hundred horses out of over two thousand had problems with their teeth or gums. A great many of these difficulties were going undetected and as a consequence, horses were often enduring a considerable amount of discomfort.

Philip trained with the American School of Equine Dentistry under the aegis of veterinarians and master dentists. A qualified equine dental technician and a member of the World Wide Association of Equine Dentistry, he didn't dispute our estimate that around a third of the horses in Julie's records appeared to be suffering from teeth troubles.

"Personally, I believe it to be higher. So many horses learn to cope with mouth problems or, like us, they're scared of the treatment and don't communicate their troubles."

Philip and Julie first met through a mutual client, Sandy, owner of Cedric, the "shoe-designing" cob. Sandy suspected her in-foal mare's teeth needed rasping but was anxious in case the stress might cause the mare to lose the foal. So, she asked Julie to be there when Philip came, to administer any necessary healing.

"I've always been interested in another dimension," said Philip. "I wasn't too sure whether or not Julie would be a waste of time, but I was prepared to look and listen. I was doing the pregnant mare's teeth without a problem, and I was just leaving when Julie told me I'd missed a bit. Well, nobody had ever said that to me before. So I challenged her. I said, 'Right, what tooth and where?' 'Towards the back and on the left hand side, on the upper teeth,' she answered. She didn't miss a beat. 'Go and have a look,' she said. I put my hand in and felt a slightly rough area. I have to say, I was surprised. But frankly, now I wish I could work with Julie eight hours a day, everyday, because I'd never need to look in a horse's mouth again—she'd just tell me the spot and I could go for it!"

The problem of horses not always communicating, or becoming so accustomed to a problem they are no longer aware of it, was highlighted by a small pony Julie was called to see.

Minty

"His owners thought this miniature Shetland wasn't eating very well," Julie said. "I did feel there was something odd about his mouth, a kind of 'locking' feeling at the back. But, he kept telling me he was fine and he wasn't in any pain. I told his owners it would be a good idea to get Philip to have a look at him, just the same."

A few days later, Philip went along to see Minty.

"I knew the pony had told Julie his teeth were okay and he was quite happy. When I looked in his mouth, his teeth had erupted into such a state that they curved up at the back and down at the front. I realised then he'd told Julie that he was okay because he'd got so used to the problem that it wasn't a worry to him—he'd never known anything else!"

Good dental care is crucial to a horse's health and well being, even if the horse himself doesn't always realise it, or welcome it. The knock-on effect of teeth problems can be considerable. It might also be said, "No teeth, no horse," on the simple premise that if a horse can't bite properly or chew well enough, he can't take in sufficient food or digest it thoroughly. Moreover, he will almost certainly try and find ways to compensate for the pain in his mouth.

"It affects them, of course it does. There are all kinds of things that might alert a horse owner to the problem: reluctance to obey commands, head-shaking, head-tilting, reluctance to move one way or the other, and 'quidding'—dropping food that they can't masticate properly. It's a long list.

"A horse with dentition problems might hold his head to one side while he's being ridden. This, in turn, may place a strain on the back, causing the horse to be totally unbalanced. He might then appear lame, but the real cause of the problem is in the mouth. Unfortunately, the horse's pain or discomfort can cause him to behave badly, which we then perceive as aggression or stubbornness. A lot of people will say 'Oh, he's being naughty,' or 'He won't cooperate,' and, very often, the root of the trouble is caused by problems with the horse's teeth. I sometimes suspect that fifty percent of behavioural problems originate in the teeth.

"I saw a three-year-old pony recently that was just coming into work and as soon as the owner tried to lunge it, it became a raving maniac. She called me in to have a look at his mouth and it appeared to have a tooth growing horizontally out of each side of his upper arcades. After a lengthy discussion with the vet, who hadn't known what the matter with the pony was either, I decided we had to sedate him and go in and have a good look.

"What I found shocked the vet, the owner, and me included! Two of his upper deciduous teeth had split, with one piece remaining rooted, and as a result, it was growing on each side. This forced it to appear as if it was growing out of the side of his mouth. I extracted no less than five caps and four split caps out of the mouth in one go. The pony has been fine ever since."

The 'caps,' remnants of baby molars or incisors, are shed at specific intervals, usually as a natural part of a horse's growing up, although if something goes amiss, they can be a source of considerable pain.

Our findings suggest that a good many horses are suffering in silence.

"I think," said Philip, "that there are an awful lot of horse owners out there who don't understand the need for proper dental maintenance. So ignorance, I suppose, is high on the list. And, of course, there's always a few who know they should—and need—to do something to help the horse, but they don't on straightforward economic grounds."

Philip has found that horses who regularly receive dental care suffer far less, and the task of putting right any problems is easier and less painful.

"Young horses, up to about the age of eight, should really be seen every six months. Older horses, the middle-aged group, if you like, between nine and twenty, can probably be seen once a year, and then when over twenty, they need checking every six months, or so. But, of course, this is just an average guide.

"The youngest horse I ever did was about eight weeks old, and that was because I was called there to see the mare. It's useful to start them from about six or seven months—that way you can pick up any misplaced teeth or other problems. Even earlier is fine. If you have a look at a foal's mouth soon after it's born, you can soon see if there are congenital abnormalities or anything likely to cause trouble. The younger you start good handling, the easier routine work will become later on. Most yearlings need their wolf teeth removed and any rough edges rasped.

"I find most horses are co-operative about the whole business. But, with maybe two out of a hundred, even when it's a standard routine procedure like rasping, you need to have the vet in so they can be sedated. Of course, if you're carrying out certain procedures, like extractions where the horse *must* be sedated, you've automatically got to have a vet on hand to administer any kind of anaesthesia.

"The hardest part of this business is an ill-mannered horse that fights me all the way and makes my job impossible, while the owner stands there saying, 'Good girl,' the whole time and I arrive home with a black eye! On the whole, I don't think what we require of horses causes them stress, so much as the way we treat them when we don't understand their needs. Horse owners who are nervous and aggressive are always inclined to block good communication with their animals—and that makes life more stressful for horses.

"Personally, I'm always very grateful for the response I get from animals that have never met me before who allow me into their space and accept the work I need to do on them. Even if they don't cooperate, I don't think physical punishment is ever acceptable. Learning to communicate without shouting is the answer, through watching and observing the horses themselves. People who don't think animals are really aware should wake up and open their eyes. Spend a day with me, and just watch. It's high time we treated animals with more respect. All animals, not just horses."

WHAT HORSES SAY

Fifty horses in the group were asked:

Are you satisfied with the way the farrier treats you?

Eighty percent had no particular problems, and the general attitude seemed to be one of acceptance.

Twenty percent had a few complaints. Some disliked, not surprisingly, *standing on three legs*. Several complained that their *shoes are too tight* and others, that the farrier was either *short tempered* or *too quick* or *impatient*.

SUMMARISING THE HORSES' VIEWPOINT

Feet, Teeth, and Pain

Having metal shoes put on your feet is not natural, essential though it may be for domesticated horses in certain conditions. Apart from the inherent difficulties for the horse, Julie has found that, for some, the metal sparks off a series of small electric shocks.

"When a horse is having this problem, I get a strong image of sparks flying and sometimes a sensation of having had a mild electric shock. For horses, it's an unpleasant tingling up their legs. They would prefer, if it were possible, to have something like cork in between the metal and their hoof. That would be a lot more comfortable for them.

"Some get these shocks from a metal bit. When they relay that to me, the best way I can describe it is to say it's like eating aluminium foil. I get a nasty taste of metal in my mouth that sets my teeth on edge. For horses, this can be even more unpleasant than getting shocks through the foot. I'd say that probably two or three out of every ten horses I see nowadays, complain about these shocks, and nearly all of them ask for a rubber bit or a much softer metal, like a copper mix."

While this particular problem is something that can be conveyed mind-to-mind, it is not easy for the horse to indicate when this is happening to him other than by his behaviour. Teeth problems are the same and tend to go unnoticed without careful observation of a horse's body language.

Anybody who's ever suffered from toothache knows what agony it can be. There's no reason to suppose that certain types of tooth problems can be any less painful for a horse, but unfortunately, the horse can't shout it out in words of one syllable. "Silence," as one trainer remarked, "is their downfall." The horse is obliged to carry on regardless, often being yanked in an already tender and sensitive mouth or ridden with a bit that might be incorrectly fitted or too harsh.

A number of horses when asked, "What do you dislike about being ridden?" found being *pulled in the mouth* particularly unpleasant, and if a horse was already suffering from teeth troubles, it added hugely to his misery. *Cold bits*, and even cold drinking water, can notch up the pain factor for horses with sensitive mouths.

"I've often seen them drinking in winter," said Julie, "and just leaving the water in their mouth so that they can warm it up first."

According to horses, we definitely need to be far more watchful. We evidently miss a lot of their signals or misinterpret quite a few that we do pick up. Questioning the horse, communicating with him at a deeper level, and making time to listen to his answers can lead to a quicker resolution of problems and far less misery for the long-suffering equine.

CHAPTER 9

Horses Never Forget

Fears, Phobias, and Frightening Experiences

Dermot

Almost like a shadow, something slithered along the floor, as quietly as a whisper. From the corner of his eye, the big grey horse caught sight of it. Held fast by four stone walls, he reared back in terror. Self-preservation took over with lightening speed. He plunged forward striking out with his front feet but heavy, shod hooves hit nothing, only a thick bed of innocent straw. Shivering, he retreated to the corner of the box. A deadly enemy was abroad. Who knew when he might strike again?

Like many people devoted to horses, Joan's equine enthusiasm began in early childhood when she fitted the end of her parents' bed with string reins and galloped off into the dawn. Her father, she said, "Got so fed up with it, he decided I'd better have riding lessons." And so it all began.

Twenty-five years ago, she bought a, "Nice grey mare to ride and to breed from." The grey turned out to be an outstanding example of an Irish Draught and became the foundation mare from whom Joan has bred four generations and more of excellent stock.

"Most of the time, I have a very good understanding with my horses, although occasionally, something happens and I'm really hard pressed to find the reason."

Dermot, who was introduced in Chapter Seven, is a handsome, grey, 17.2 hand home-bred Irish Draught-Thoroughbred cross who Joan describes as a "big wimp," his size and strength often appearing in contrast to his sometimes timid nature. One spring, he was being schooled at a local equestrian centre and was due to be ridden in the four-year-old hunter class at the county show.

Joan set off at the wheel of her heavyweight horsebox to collect Dermot and take him to make his first show ring appearance. When she arrived at the equestrian centre, one of the grooms reported that the horse seemed to have got himself in a bit of a state.

"Apparently," Joan recounted, "he'd been waiting in the stable, all kitted up with his rug, roller, and tailguard, ready to go in the horsebox. Then suddenly, they heard an almighty crashing and banging."

When the groom went to investigate, there was Dermot, standing in the middle of the stable, with no roller and no tailguard.

"None of us could imagine what had happened. We could only suppose that somehow or other he'd caught the roller on the edge of the manger, and panicked. Anyway, by the time I got there, he seemed to have calmed down. So we rugged him up in a different one, and put on his travelling boots but no tailguard because it had been broken along with the roller."

Dermot went up into the horsebox without any fuss, but his air of calm and tranquillity wasn't destined to last for long.

"About half a mile down the road, he went absolutely berserk. The horsebox was rocking from side-to-side and I was hanging on to the steering wheel for dear life. I honestly thought the whole thing was going to turn over and that horsebox is no lightweight. I've never experienced anything like it. Never. Not in twenty-five years of transporting my horses around. Anyway, I stopped and pulled over as quickly as I could. There was a man just up the road, gully-emptying. He stood there with his mouth wide open, looking at us."

This was hardly the moment to leap into the horsebox or start hauling down ramps, so Joan stood outside, quietly talking to Dermot and trying to calm him down.

"After what seemed like an eternity," she said, "the kicking got a bit less hysterical. I decided to get into the horsebox by the rear groom's door. It would have been too dangerous to get in front with Dermot."

Over the top of the high partition, Joan could see that the horse was no longer wearing a rug.

"It was on the floor in rags and tatters. I didn't know what to do—carry on or go home. In the end, I thought I might as well carry on, as by now, Dermot had calmed down considerably and was picking at his hay net."

They managed to get to the show in one piece with only one more episode of kicking as they neared the entrance to the showground. When Joan took down the ramp she was at a loss for words.

"I couldn't believe my eyes. Dermot had kicked the horsebox so hard that the window had fallen out, and he was standing amidst broken glass, the window grill, his rug, and completely shredded back-leg travelling boots. The bottom fixings for the back and side partitions had been sheared off, and there were deep gouges in the partitions and outside panel. Even his back shoes, which had been put on just the day before had shifted, he'd kicked so violently. It was unbelievable. Later on, when I had an estimate for repairing the horsebox, the damage came to over £2000. Thank goodness the horsebox had been so strong, otherwise it might have been a very different story."

Luckily, their farrier was on the showground and he refitted the hind shoes and Dermot went on to be ridden in the hunter class.

"He was reasonably calm by this stage, but it was his first show and a big class. When the judge rode him, he got jabbed in the mouth and kicked in the ribs. Poor old Dermot just froze because he didn't know what to do. He certainly didn't give a very good ride, but then, that was hardly his fault. All in all, it was a bit of a disaster. And, of course, we still had absolutely no idea what had upset him."

Not surprisingly, Dermot wasn't keen to get back in the horsebox. Joan wisely decided to transport him with no boots, bandages, or rugs.

"On the way back home, he was so quiet you wouldn't have known he was there."

The mystery remained unsolved until some weeks later, when Julie came to give Dermot healing. It was a complex tale that unfolded bit by bit. Dermot related to Julie, through images and the inner voice, what had happened.

"It seems that on the morning of the show," said Julie, "Dermot thought he'd seen a brown snake in his stable and it frightened him. Then, he said, the snake jumped on his back, which is why he'd panicked in the stable. I asked him if the snake went when he got the roller off and he said, *yes*. Then, he said the snake was in the horsebox, around his hind legs. I asked him if the snake went when he got the rug off, and he said, *yes, and it nearly scared me to death*."

Julie and Joan gave this explanation a good deal of thought and finally deduced what had happened to cause Dermot so much misery. At the equestrian centre, when the groom came to prepare Dermot for travelling to the show, she had put on his rug with a roller and tailguard.

While she was doing this, Dermot had his headcollar on and was tied up. The groom then untied him and took the rope off. When she left the stable, she also left the rope behind, coiled up just inside the door. According to Joan and Julie, this must have been the moment when Dermot first took fright.

"We reckoned," Joan said, "that Dermot thought that the coiled-up rope on the stable floor was a snake. He went into panic, caught the roller on the manger, which then pulled the roller sideways. That, in turn, pulled the strap on the tail guard tight, and he must have convinced himself that this was 'a snake on his back.' Of course, it would make sense that the 'snake' would disappear once the roller straps had broken and the roller and tail guard had fallen off."

After this mishap, Dermot had been given a different rug to travel in, which didn't need a roller. This rug was slightly on the small side, with a fillet string that fitted quite snugly along his sides and at the back of his hind legs. When he had been loaded into the horsebox, although much calmer, he was still upset by the incident in the stable.

"I think somehow or other," said Joan, "after the horsebox had travelled a little way, Dermot must have suddenly noticed the pressure of the fillet string around his sides and hind legs, and not being able to turn round and see what it was, he must have decided it was the snake attacking him again. This was obviously enough to send him berserk—and that's why he began kicking the horsebox to pieces."

Julie took up the story.

"I was talking to the groom who'd been looking after Dermot," she recalled. "The groom told me that she'd left the rope coiled-up by the door the morning of the show. She also told me that she'd seen snakes several times at the stables. It looked as if Dermot had probably seen a real snake at some point, maybe even on the morning of the show. It might have been in his box, or maybe, he just saw it in the yard. Anyway, he was clearly terrified by the whole business and it was quite difficult to ask him any more about it. I gave him healing, and he seemed much better."

Joan observed that the whole experience had left its mark on Dermot.

"A couple of years after the snake incident he still hadn't forgotten about it. One day, I was bringing all the horses into the yard for their feeds.

I usually take several headcollars to the gate and throw them onto the bales of hay that I'm putting out.

"As Dermot came through the gate, he suddenly froze and stared with a terrified look on his face towards the hay bales. When I turned round to see what had caused such a reaction, I saw that where I'd thrown the headcollars onto the bale, one of the ropes was trailing on the ground, towards the gate. It was a brown rope and judging by the violence of his reaction, he must have thought it was another snake. Even today, although he's used to wearing all sorts of rugs, Dermot won't travel in the horsebox with a rug on."

"Horses," Julie remarked, "consider snakes highly dangerous. I know that if they've ever been frightened or bitten by one, they don't forget it in a hurry. That is, if they ever do forget. I worked with one horse who had an appalling bite and it was touch-and-go whether he was going to live. He'd been out in the field and, somehow or other, had trodden on the snake by mistake. The vet was called immediately, and he came out and gave the horse painkillers. The puncture wound was just below the hock, on the fetlock. By the time I got to see him, the hind leg was enormous and the swelling had almost reached the stifle. The vet told me that if the swelling went any further, the horse would die

"The heat coming from the leg was incredible. It was like holding your hands near a red hot stove. He was in terrible agony but he responded brilliantly to healing. I think it took about six weeks for his mobility to come back and he's completely sound now. But, his owner says he tends to shy at things in the road a lot more often, especially anything that reminds him at all of a snake—like bits of wire or a twisty green plant."

Ozzie

There was a small window, set up high just above a bank. Inside, the stable sloped away. It was dark, and the mare hated the smell of pigs that wafted across

the yard. Whenever she was put in there, something bad happened. She had been sick and they had put her in the stable. But, they didn't know that it was the stable that made her even worse. The man with a white coat came often to see her. They held her very tightly with a thick rope and then they put something down her throat that hurt. She knew when they were coming because she could see the boots out of the window. Sometimes, after the men left the stable, they stood talking to one another outside the narrow window—even when the boots finally moved away, she was still afraid.

When Pat and her husband bought their daughter a fourteen-year-old Thoroughbred mare called Ozzie, she had already been evented up to intermediate level.

From the beginning, it was clear that she was a mare who had her own special problems. The first indication came when the vet arrived to give Ozzie her routine injections.

"She went absolutely crazy," said Pat. "We couldn't get near her and I honestly thought she was going to kill the pair of us. The vet managed in the end by injecting her in the shoulder instead of the neck. A year later, we had got used to her ways, and she to ours, and I think Ozzie was settling down well. She wasn't too brilliant with men, though, apart from my husband, Carl, who she'd taken a great liking to. When it came time, a year later, for her to have her injections again, we went through the same terrifying performance when the vet came into her stable. Again, she just went crazy.

"Then, for some reason—I honestly don't know what made me come out with it—I said to the vet that maybe it was his green wellington boots, perhaps that's what she hates. 'Right,' he said. 'If you think it's the wellies, I'll go and put my shoes on.' He came back wearing shoes and she still wasn't very happy, but at least she accepted his presence and we were able to give her the injections a good deal more easily. There was obviously some link but I didn't know for sure what it was."

Pat and Carl put the incident out of their mind until two years later when, on a pouring wet autumn day, Carl went to get the horses in. As usual, he was carrying a headcollar and carrots, which was normally enough for Ozzie to come up and be caught without difficulty.

"The rain was tipping down but Carl couldn't catch her. She went off snorting and blowing and wouldn't come anywhere near him. He came back in, absolutely dripping wet from head to toe, saying he couldn't think what on earth had got into her. Then all of a sudden, it clicked. I looked down at his feet and, of course, he was wearing wellies, green wellies! I thought maybe that's why he couldn't catch her. So I went out in my shoes and caught her without any problem. Normally, neither of us would ever wear wellies, just 'muckers,' or shoes. I really began to wonder if the green boots were a definite trigger."

Pat was more than a little curious about why Ozzie seemed so disturbed by what was normally just harmless footwear.

"After we bought the mare, we did manage to track down most of her history, but there were two years that were a blank, and it was obviously in those years that the trauma had begun. So the next time Julie came out, I asked if she could have a go with Ozzie and find out the story of the green wellies and what lay behind it."

"She told me," Julie recalled, "that she'd been kept in a cow shed, deep in mud. She was by herself and there was a window that she could look through but it was more or less at ground level. When she looked out of the window, she could see people wearing green wellies coming towards her. Whenever she saw that, something really bad happened. It looked as though she'd been pushed up into a corner and injected."

There was still further evidence several years later as Pat reported.

"I was very glad to find out what had happened to Ozzie. But it was impossible to wipe out her memory of whatever was done to her when she was shut up. A year or more after Julie confirmed the business about the wellies, our farrier came out to shoe Ozzie. Normally, she was very good. I was holding on to her when I had to answer the phone, so I asked Carl to come and hold her. She started misbehaving, although there was nothing happening in the shoeing to upset her. It was only afterwards, we suddenly realised what it must have been. Carl had been wearing green wellies again."

Five years after being in a loving and gentle home, the sight of a pair of green wellington boots was enough to trigger off a violent reaction. Equine memory is indeed remarkable.

"'Ozzie,' said Julie, "isn't the only horse that's complained of being shut in a small dark place. One horse I was giving healing to, a champion stallion, gave me a very clear picture of being shut up in a small shed. It frightened him nearly to death. It was done because the trainer he was with at the time considered that shutting him up in darkness would make him quieter and more obedient. Nothing could have been worse for him, especially as he'd hit his head going into the stable, or shed as he saw it.

"The poor horse was almost ill with fear, and it took him a long time to get over that experience. It seemed to stay at the back of his mind for years. In the end, though, he did respond well to healing."

Pablo

Mary is an experienced horsewoman of many years standing. Trained as a zoologist, much of her work has been to concentrate on farm animal and equine behaviour. One incident that puzzled her concerned her dapple-grey gelding, Pablo, who, when he was about ten, had suddenly developed an extraordinary dislike for one of her garments.

"I'd had this green fleece since new. I suppose I'd worn it for quite a long time, several months or more, before the trouble started. One day, I went out in the field to get Pablo in the way I always do. No chance! I think it was the first time ever that he refused to come in. He just snorted, went into reverse, and shot off down the field. Sometimes, of course, if there's lots of grass in the field, he'll ignore me and then wander over later. It's sort of a game, really. But this business was quite different. I eventually caught him and realised that it must be the fleece because there was no problem when I wasn't wearing it."

Julie tried to find out why there'd been such an abrupt change in Pablo's usual behaviour.

"Pablo said that she smelled odd when she was wearing it. It was the right hand side of the fleece between the chest and shoulder that according to Pablo, just went 'Phew.' He thought, *I'm not having that, it's really weird.* If she had it on when she was riding, it reminded him of wind going through dry leaves. At first, he didn't like the smell, then there were bits in the material that rustled, and he didn't like the sound."

WHAT HORSES SAY

We wanted to know what kind of experiences were not just alarming but so deeply frightening they left their mark. We also wanted to know how horses felt about travelling, as this was evidently a potential source of stress for some. The whole group of sixty-two was questioned on frightening experiences, and forty-five on travelling.

What is the most frightening thing that's ever happened to you?
Some of these events went very deep indeed and may have affected the horse's behaviour if not permanently, at least for a considerable length of time. Although every animal's experience was unique, there were certain events that commonly occurred. The main categories involved some form of falling or being unable to get up, separation anxiety from being loaded into a horsebox, and leaving their mother. The remainder of the group had

experiences that ranged from losing a companion to having stomach ache. For each horse, the memory of the event was still new.

Falling

Forty percent of the group rated some kind of fall, or being stuck or cornered, as their most frightening experience. They reported: *fell over and couldn't get up; fell over on right side and put out right shoulder; flipped and went over; fell and bashed nose; slipped in field; fell over in horsebox; slipped with hind legs, getting legs under belly; reared and went over backwards; did splits with front legs and hurt knee; lay down in stable and couldn't get up; got back legs caught in wire; got stuck in bog in deep mud.*

Separation

Eighteen percent considered some form of separation their most frightening experience: *being taken away; carted off; being alone.* The answers were truly poignant. For almost all of them, this separation involved going in a horsebox or trailer for the first time, and this, allied with the harshness of separation from their mother or companion, was a truly traumatic experience.

Leaving Mother

Eleven percent specifically regarded separation from their mother as their most frightening experience. *Suddenly she was gone* was the commonest response. Broodmares reported *losing sight of their foal* or *foal being taken away* as deeply frightening, which again serves to point out how distressing this event can be if it's not handled with compassion and understanding, as was illustrated in Chapter Three.

Other Responses

Six percent reported that *being blindfolded* or *having a bag put over their heads* had been truly terrifying.

Six percent said that being *hit on the head* or *shut up alone in a dark place* had been their worst experience.

Nineteen percent—the remainder of the group—had a variety of individual experiences that they regarded as their most frightening. They included: *cold; hunger; injections; stomach ache; running a race; losing a companion; noseband too tight and unable to breathe; smoke; cart out of control* and *put in a starting stall.*

Do you like travelling in a horsebox or trailer?

Sixty-seven percent of horses questioned did not like the experience. One horse summed up transport by reporting: *dislike everything about it!* However, there was common agreement that *slippery floors; fast braking; steep ramps; being shut in; lack of space; not seeing where you're going* and *being thrown about* were unpleasant aspects of being transported.

Thirty-three percent rated it from *enjoy it* to *okay.* The main criteria for these horses appeared to be what was going to happen when they stepped down the ramp. For those who were going to shows or events that they enjoyed, the horsebox was seen as a means to an agreeable end.

SUMMARISING THE HORSES' VIEWPOINT

Fears, Phobias, and Frightening Experiences

There's nothing new about the variety of things that can frighten a horse. From innocent plastic bags in the hedgerow to a ten-ton tractor filling up the lane, from a snake in the grass to a scarf around the neck, the list can be almost as long as anyone cares to make it. What interested us was to discover what horses themselves considered to be not just merely alarming, but deeply frightening.

Some experiences, especially those that involved some form of falling, could have had considerable repercussions on their whole anatomy, and were physical as well as emotional in their after effects.

In horse transport, it seems that there are still improvements to be made, especially in the matter of over-steep ramps, slippery floors, and fast braking. It should certainly never be forgotten that for a flight animal to be cooped up in a small, darkish, moving space is utterly against every aspect of its nature.

"Frankly," said Julie, "I'd like to see everyone who has anything to do with transporting animals experience what it's like to ride in the back of a horsebox or trailer, just as if you were that animal. Of course, I know it would have to be under controlled conditions, but I think it would make people be a lot more understanding of what horses and farm animals have to put up with."

Do horses ever forget a frightening event? Since they are so individual, as even our brief survey showed, it's hard to know the answer to this. Certainly some, like Liam or Barouche or Ozzie, never forgot, even in the hands of patient and understanding owners. It took little to trigger off a response to an old and frightening memory, even years after the actual event. Others, like Lucy in Chapter Four, appeared able to integrate the experience and not be permanently damaged by it. Still others, perhaps, try simply to block off bad memories.

Fear certainly seems to lies at the root of most horses' behavioural problems. It is a fact that in horse-human relationships, fear has an unfortunately large part to play on both sides. The horse is badly frightened by something, which, to human eyes and ears, is either non-existent or so trivial that it couldn't possibly be regarded as fearsome. For instance, to a horse whose eyes are geared to peripheral vision and who has no natural understanding of depth, a five-centimetre puddle may be five metres deep and dangerous, for all he knows.

As an essentially timid creature and flight animal, the horse naturally uses running away as the first form of defence—with potentially serious consequences to the rider. The rider, in turn, becomes frightened and in the grip of fear often acts no more wisely than the horse. If a horse can't take to his heels and get away from what scares him, then inevitably, he deals with it as best he can, which sometimes means displaying behaviour that the human being regards as aggressive and threatening.

Consequently, in a mixture of fear, anger, and self-defence, the human strikes back. This particular scenario is even more common when humans are dealing with a larger-than-average, feisty horse upon whom they are intent on imposing their will, no matter what. If an animal resists their wishes, the consequences for the horse can often be grim. In Julie's records of over two thousand horses, almost four hundred reported that, at some point, they had a *blow to the head* and consequently suffered *headaches*.

Saddest of all, frequently the reason for a horse's so-called "bad" behaviour is something that has terrified the animal but is inexplicable to the owner, as was the case with Ozzie and the green wellington boots, and with Dermot and the appearance, real or imagined, of a snake in the horsebox.

If human beings don't understand what makes a horse react as he does, the responsibility rests squarely with us to try and uncover the cause. A lack of communication between horse and human can easily bring about a whole chain of unhappy and painful consequences, sometimes almost as much for the human as for the horse.

"Horses," said Julie, "are very generous. They seldom blame us for what happens to them. They don't seem to judge us."

Fortunately for us, horses are surprisingly forgiving creatures. However, it is in the area of the often "mysterious" fears that a deeper and more profound kind of communication can be used, which may well help bring the answer to the surface.

Horse Sense and Sensibility

Emotions and Understanding

LISTEN OR YOUR TONGUE WILL MAKE YOU DEAF

Cherokee saying

B y common definition, "horse sense" is synonymous with practical intelligence: know-how, common sense, mother-wisdom, and just plain good sense. The expression may have its origins in describing the horsemen of the American west, but it can also apply to the nature of horses themselves.

Horses have a clearer idea of what's best for them and what they want than is generally believed. Horses read our body language and do so very successfully much of the time. In fact, they appear a good deal better at reading the subtleties in ours than we are at reading theirs. They also have a well-developed ability to sense what people are thinking and feeling. Their problem is how to communicate this.

When human beings are willing to make a quantum leap and interact with horses on a mental or energetic level, it becomes possible to start discovering what wisdom and feeling exists in the depths of the equine mind. Clear lines of communication, whether it's between human beings or between humans and animals, can make the difference between misery and happiness. Simple failure to understand one another is probably responsible for more anguish than almost anything else—not just in the human domain but in the relationship between horses and humans.

Horse sense and sensitivity extend over a range of sometimes unexpected areas. In this chapter, we shall look at horses' awareness of their names, their ability to self-medicate, their capacity to show concern for our well being, and how their acute sense of smell can affect their behaviour.

Brenda and Maureen

No one bats an eyelid over a dog who knows his own name. In fact, it's expected that a dog should know what he's called. As for horses, a name, it appears, might have just as much influence on them. Some names certainly appear to be appreciated more than others.

When Julie and her family first moved to a small farm, she inherited a couple of aged, ex-racehorses. The horses had always lived out, never been rugged up, and were not overly friendly towards strangers. One of the mares was almost blind and was wholly reliant upon her friend, who acted as leader and made sure she safely negotiated her way around the field. One afternoon, just a few weeks after Julie had undertaken the care of the two old mares, she was aware of one of them staring intently at her.

"I heard her say, *I want to be called Brenda*," Julie recalled. "I told her I was sure she didn't. Back came the answer, *Yes, I do*. I thought, well, if that's really what would make you happy, okay. I don't have a problem with that. The next thing I heard was the other mare saying, *I want to be called Maureen*. I told her that was fine, too, and we'll call you whatever you want. The names they'd been given were typical racing names that made no sense at all. Anyway, I went off and moved some bales on the far side of the barn. Then I called out, 'Brenda.'

"She was munching her hay and looked up at once, and whinnied. Off I went and came back about twenty minutes later, and called, 'Maureen,' and sure enough, she looked up, too, and whinnied, just as the other mare had done. So I told them it was absolutely okay, and from that moment on, they'd be Brenda and Maureen. They both just stood there and nodded."

The mares, it should be said, had never once taken the slightest bit of notice when they had been called by their old names. Getting the nod, quite literally, from Brenda and Maureen, is not uncommon. A lot of horse owners have seen their horses nodding and find it rather "sweet," but often think it's some sort of behavioural twitch, rather than the possibility of a conscious, positive response. However, Julie has learned that in a great number of cases, a horse nodding his head is doing exactly what he appears to be—saying *yes*.

Mabel

Brenda and Maureen are by no means an isolated example of how horses feel about their names.

British Horse Society instructor Samantha, with a lifetime's experience of working professionally with horses, once owned a Warmblood mare called Mabel.

"I always wondered if she really liked her name," Samantha said. "She had a reputation as quite a difficult horse with other people, but we got along very well and she learned to trust me. At one session, she told Julie that she really disliked the name Mabel and wanted to be called Misty. I was very happy to call her what she wanted."

We saw earlier in Chapter Five, how the black mare, Stella, had appreciated her new name. She had believed that her name was "Stupid." It is not clear if she knew what the word meant.

"I don't know the answer to this one, either," said Julie. "I do know that some horses very definitely understand the meaning of words, but whether they know it from the tone of voice or whether they've been told by another horse, I can't be sure. Some are much smarter than others. But, most are definitely aware of what they're called.

"I remember one horse who had been renamed Mystique, and her new owner wanted to know if she liked her name. The mare was quite happy about it. The owner was curious to find out whether or not the mare knew what her old name had been. The mare told me she'd been known as Holly."

Her new owner nearly fell over with astonishment. Holly had indeed been the mare's name in her former home.

Bill

Horses' sensibilities go beyond recognition of their names. Awareness of what is good for them and what they require extends not just from an ability, in some horses, to assess the kind of shoes they need, but also an awareness of what sort of food is best suited to their particular body and digestive system. In short, horses very often know the solution to their problems—if asked.

Eve is the granddaughter of Jane, the professional dealer who we met in Chapter Eight. Eve also works in the family business and keeps her own special horse, Bill, on the yard. The black, three-quarter Thoroughbred and quarter Shire gelding suddenly began windsucking and getting frequent bouts of colic.

"He was in quite a bad way," said Julie, "he would pace round his box like crazy—there were marks up the wall where he'd been kicking, trying to ease the pain. His mood was miserable because he felt so bad."

Bill's diet had included haylage and sugar beet, a regime that suits many horses extremely well and helps them to maintain good condition.

"He told me that his food was too rich for him. It gave him awful bellyache and that was why he kept windsucking. It was like a human with acute indigestion who needs to burp to relieve the trapped wind. Horses can't burp, of course, but it was what Bill was trying to do through wind-sucking. He said it helped relieve the pain in his stomach. He asked for slippery elm twice a day for his stomach, and chamomile tea and goose grass clivers—as well as apple chaff and a probiotic. We obliged him!"

His diet was changed, no more haylage or sugar beet and back to hay and a simple ready made horse mix.

Eve considered, "His colic had been so bad, I'm not sure how many attacks he could have survived. But the healing and the change of diet Bill suggested to Julie altered everything. I think it saved his life."

Bill continues as a super family horse, a quiet and capable all-rounder.

"He's not the only horse, by any means, that has a problem with allergies to certain foods," said Julie. "I've found quite a few can't digest haylage easily. Some of them eat it very fast. They don't have to chew it so much, the way they do with hay. They don't produce enough saliva and digestive juices so when it hits the stomach, it's harder for them to digest."

Jerry

Horses are good at taking their medicine, especially if they find it themselves. Laura, Garth's owner, used to have an elderly pony called Jerry.

"He was a dear old thing and had been Amy's first pony. Julie came to treat him for his arthritis. For quite a while, whenever I'd been bringing him back from the field, he would snatch at some bracken as we passed the hedgerow. I always tried to pull him away as I was certain bracken was very poisonous for horses. He only did it when the bracken was fresh and green—around June and July."

When questioned by Julie, Jerry came up with the answer.

"He told me that he only ever took just four leaves, never more. He said it helped his arthritis and his worms, if he ever had any."

Mervyn and Denys

Mervyn and Denys belonged to a retired teacher, Anthea. Anthea has ridden for pleasure since early childhood and has become increasingly interested in observing horse behaviour.

"There was a period a few years back when Mervyn really wasn't very well," said Anthea. "There was nothing dramatic. It was more a question of simply not being on form. Our vet, Jonathan, came out and did all the usual blood and urine tests, and nothing showed up. A friend of mine suggested that I ask Julie to come and see Mervyn. I gave her absolutely no information about him other than his age and breed. I just told her that he wasn't himself.

"She immediately told me that he had a bit of arthritis in his shoulders, which was to be expected at his age. Then, she put her hands over the middle of his back and said, 'Oh, this is hot—his kidneys aren't very good at all,' and gave him healing. He had some requests, too, and asked to be given honey and dark seaweed and nettle tea. Within a week, there was a big difference, and within a fortnight, he was back to his old self, nineteen going on four!"

Anthea had also invested in a younger horse, Denys, who had mysteriously begun to lose all the hair down the left side of his face and behind his ears. There seemed to be no obvious cause. Anthea asked Julie to come and see if she could find the answer.

"Denys told Julie that he was allergic to lanolin and beeswax—stuff that's in tack-cleaning creams. He wanted a sheepskin covering over his bridle. Julie told him he couldn't have sheepskin because it had lanolin in it. We put our heads together and thought that a synthetic sheepskin might be the answer.

"I cleaned his bridle very carefully so there were no traces of lanolin left, and I got a synthetic sheepskin specially made for it. Within a week or two, the hair on Denys's face had grown back. He was just fine again."

"I remember," Julie added, "that he particularly wanted his face bathed in water that had Bach Flower crab apple essence added to it. He wanted crab apple in his water, too, and cider-apple vinegar, sunflower oil, and vitamin E capsules, and vitamin E cream on his face."

These requests are defined by the horse through a series of questions, answers, and visual images, as well as the presentation of specific items to the horse, so that the animal is able to convey to Julie exactly what he wants.

Anthea has found that Julie's visits and her ability to communicate clearly what the horses need has brought about a change in her own attitude.

"I'm much more careful about what I think and what I say when I'm around the horses now and how I say things, too. I listen to them much more and try and get on the same wavelength."

Liddie and Becca

Soon after their first meeting at the equine clinic, Josie asked Julie to come and have a look at one of her own horses, a 16 hand, black Thoroughbred mare called Liddie.

"Liddie was rising six when she went to a friend's farm where she was being trained to event," said Josie. "I knew her back was hurting her, her coat wasn't right, and she was rather grumpy. She was normally a kind mare, but she wasn't improving in her work and she kept making the same mistakes over and over again. Her sire was a talented but complex horse, who had produced some real head bangers—what a colleague of mine used to call 'migraine horses'— the kind that whatever you do, they never seemed to get any better."

Julie relayed what the mare wanted.

"To my amazement," Josie said, "the mare asked for grapefruit. I couldn't believe she would want grapefruit, let alone eat it. We offered her peeled grapefruit, but she ate the lot—flesh, skin, and pips, and she wanted grapefruit essential oil rubbed on her left side, on the point of the buttock. When you did that she'd drift off into a soporific state."

Grapefruit is not perhaps the first thing that would leap to mind and certainly not likely to do so in the normal course of veterinary diagnosis. But, the mare had sent Julie a clear picture of the large, round yellow fruit, and the moment grapefruit was offered, Liddie seized it with alacrity. Grapefruit is not likely to be found in the list of equine foodstuffs or preferences. It certainly isn't handed out as some tasty titbit. Nor does it grow in hedgerows, fields, or at the edge of stable yards—but, it was undoubtedly what Liddie needed.

"Looking at the pharmaceutical properties," Judith considered, "might tell you grapefruit has a calming influence. But why should a horse ask for a citrus fruit that isn't grown in this country? It's not something horses would normally have access to. I suppose she could have picked up the smell on me at some time or other, and she may have derived a benefit. The farm where she'd been stabled when she was in training used to put bits and pieces on a heap and burn them, so maybe she found some leftover grapefruit in the field. I don't know. I can't square it. But I accept it.

"I had a much better understanding with Liddie after Julie's ministrations, and we got over her problems. She's sold now and doing really well. In fact, she won an intermediate event just recently."

Becca, Josie's Irish Draught mare, also developed a particular fondness for one special item although it was less unusual than grapefruit.

"One spring," Josie said, "Becca got azoturia and I asked Julie to have a look at her. Julie found out she wanted dandelions. Not just the leaves, but the whole heads. As soon as I turned her out, she'd make a beeline for the dandelions and stuff herself with them, flower heads and all, then go and eat grass."

Sula

Horses are far more aware of our feelings than we often give them credit for, as Garth revealed in Chapter Five when he made special efforts to take care of Amy. Carriage driving enthusiast Patsy discovered a depth of concern in her pony, Sula, which quite astonished her.

Patsy has been a regular competitor in local driving events for many years, often with Sula, an excellent, strawberry-roan mare. Patsy's granddaughter, Jennie, simply adored the pony, and whenever she visited her grandmother she spent hours in the stable with Sula.

"On one occasion," said Patsy, "when I'd asked Julie to come out and give the ponies a check over, she said that there was a message for me from Sula. The pony had told her she'd had a young visitor at the weekend and wanted to know if everything was okay because she'd banged her left leg, just above the knee. At first, I was puzzled by this very odd message. What visitor? Then I remembered that Jennie had been staying with us. The next time I saw my granddaughter I said, 'Did you hurt yourself at all on Sunday when you came up to see us?'

"She immediately said yes and that she'd banged her leg on Sula's stable door. I asked her which leg she'd hurt. She said it was the left one, just above the knee. I realised then exactly what must have happened. I'd hung a wet hay net inside the stable door to drain. When young Jennie had opened the door to go in and see Sula, the weight of the hay net must have forced the door to bang back against her leg. I knew that pony absolutely adored Jennie and had looked after her from day one. But even so I was absolutely 'gobsmacked.'"

Cedric

The scent of young Jennie may have played a part in Sula's devotion to her. Smell is, for many horses, the first form of communication, the first step in assessing whether we're the kind of people they want near them—or not.

Cedric, the "wise old sage" who was rather good designing his own shoes in Chapter Eight, had clear ideas on other matters as well, and on one visit, gave Julie a few difficulties in interpreting his views. She recalled a day when the cob made a most unexpected statement.

"He's a very chatty horse. He comes out with all sorts of things, often about what's troubling the other horses or who's got worms. On one visit, he wanted to tell us about the fox that was coming through the yard in the middle of the night, winding them all up. He's usually got his head out over the stable door talking away before I even get to him.

"He's very affectionate towards Sandy, his owner, too. But this time, he was quite withdrawn, and when Sandy and I approached him, he reversed to the back of the box. He was quite subdued and not like his usual self at all.

"I asked him what was wrong. He said, straightaway, *Sandy stinks!* I was really taken aback and I was desperately wondering how on earth I was going to put this. I asked him to explain a bit more. He said that she *smelled different* and *much stronger*, and he didn't like it at all. It wasn't her normal smell, and it was obviously making him very uneasy. I asked Sandy if she'd done anything different, like changing her shampoo or deodorant. It turned out that she'd just bought some rather expensive duty-free perfume. She fancied it smelled pretty good."

Definitely not to Cedric. To keep him happy, Sandy obligingly returned to her old perfume, and Cedric returned to his happy, chatty self. However, he was not the only horse to complain when his sense of smell was offended. Abe, who belonged to British Horse Society instructor Sally, had a point to make.

Abe
Julie had been out to do a final check on Abe, introduced in Chapter Seven, to make quite sure some minor adjustments to his saddle were to his com-

plete satisfaction. Abe was happy with the saddle but had one or two other comments to make. While she was in the stable with Abe, an elderly Border collie called Jim, one of the four owned by the family, was sitting outside the door.

"Old Jim was going on like anything," said Julie. "He was saying that bloody horse was always moaning. It was too hot, too cold, and if Abe had done as much work as he, Jim, had done in his life, he'd have something to bloody well moan about! I tell you, it was absolutely comic. Anyway, Abe was quite annoyed and fed up because there was a smell he hated. He wanted the dead cow removed as soon as possible."

Investigation revealed that Sally's father had discovered a dead cow out in the woods. It had been brought, temporarily, to a field behind the stable, some distance from Abe. It was far enough away to be undetectable by a human nose, but it was strong and unpleasant to a horse's highly sensitive nostrils.

∞

At one stud farm, the local vet came to take a blood sample from a Thoroughbred gelding who was inclined to be difficult. When Julie questioned the horse, it seemed that the horse disliked *the way the vet smelled*. This seemed to trouble the gelding more than the procedure itself. Julie suggested the vet apply lavender oil before taking the blood sample. Somewhat sceptically, he agreed, but later commented that the whole business had been easier than usual.

Equine vet Josie has observed that some mares have a particular dislike of tobacco smoke and react quite violently to it. She has also encountered a mare who had such a strong dislike of beer that when approached by a young man smelling heavily of it, actually bit off the tip of his nose.

On the other side of the coin, one stallion became so enchanted with the scent of the head girl at the stud, that he was one the verge of becoming a real nuisance to her.

"The stallion," said Julie, "thought she smelled just wonderful."

Garth's adoration of Amy was centred upon the way she smelled, and it's a theme that appears to be echoed regularly by equines everywhere.

Everyone knows that sometimes just a whiff of say, garlic, can carry us instantly to a Paris restaurant. Or less agreeably, a hint of overboiled cabbage can be a sudden reminder of school food. If our sense of smell, vastly limited in comparison with a horse's, can affect us so powerfully, its influence on a horse must be amazing.

Julie has observed that when she's working on horses whose skin gives off what she describes as an "unpleasant cheesy smell, a bit like overripe brie," they would often have some form of liver or stomach problems. Josie has remarked on the bias that one of her stallions had towards the scent of grey mares, while another favoured chestnuts, and a third disliked piebald or skewbald mares.

Anyone with a reasonably developed sense of smell (and not worried about being considered eccentric!) can detect a difference in odour between say, a dark bay, a chestnut, and a grey, particularly if he or she cares to sniff close to the withers where horses naturally groom one another. The darker the colour, the stronger the smell. On a coloured horse, the white areas smell quite different from the brown or black sections.

If the smell is obvious to us, "scent-dumb" humans, what must it be like for a horse? Could this be one of the reasons why some horses don't like their piebald or skewbald stablemates? Or, appear hostile to a particular horse? If we, who are more or less "scent-challenged" can detect differences, smell has got to be crucial for a horse.

WHAT HORSES SAY

All sixty-two horses and ponies were asked about the role smell plays in communicating with us, their own ability to sense our emotions, and whether they could help us communicate better with them.

What sense do you use most in communicating with us?
Eighty percent relied on *smell* as the primary sense in their communication with us.

Six percent used *smell* primarily and *visual* as their secondary sense.

Five percent relied principally on *visual* sense.

Five percent used *visual* principally and rated *smell* as a secondary sense.

Three percent rated *taste* as important and wanted to be able to lick the person.

One percent considered *smell* as their principal sense but also wanted to *touch*.

Can you sense what people are feeling? How?
One hundred percent of the horses answered *yes*, to the question of whether they could sense our feelings. There appeared to be no doubt that they all, in varying degrees, were able to pick up our emotional state. Some, understandably, didn't always find the experience pleasant.

How horses sensed our feelings, though, was more complex, and gave rise to sixty-two different answers. Because of the highly individual variations, the horses' responses are not expressed in percentages, but simply in themes:

Bad Moods
Anger and irritation seems to be conveyed to horses very fast indeed, which is a sobering point for the quick-tempered amongst us. The answers were

individual but covered similar themes: *know when angry because person gives off a buzz; uncomfortable; dislike agitated feeling so block off; can sense but block off; don't like aggression; especially sense aggravation; especially sense anger; can sense if agitated; if cross, prickly; especially sense when angry; especially sense when stressed.*

Waves of Emotion

Horses were quite specific about how they picked up our signals. For most, our feelings were revealed to them through a wide variety of different ways: *person gives off waves; by warmth; by smell; by atmosphere; look and know; there's an electric charge; feel by energy system.* A few simply responded that, for them, it was *just a feeling.* Horses evidently have no difficulty in sensing our emotional state, with some equines having a very sophisticated warning system.

Two horses out of the group were inclined to be particularly kind if they sensed unhappiness and tried to offer *comfort* or, *if sad, like to come into person's space and show love.*

It certainly looks as if we need to do a better job of sorting out our own emotional state if we want to improve our relationship with horses. The gelding who responded *dislike agitated feeling from person, and block off,* may well be the sort of horse who, when his rider gets cross, becomes zombie-like in order to avoid the unpleasant sensations he's picking up.

Can you teach us to communicate better with you?

Eighty-seven percent of the horses and ponies gave an unqualified *yes,* when asked if they could teach us to communicate better. Thirteen percent of the group didn't know how this could be done, but the overwhelming majority felt there was some help they could offer us. Their advice had three principal themes: *observe; be patient;* and *listen.* Two horses, especially, urged us to *see the picture*, and work *mind-to-mind, send pictures*. It is advice that we will look at in greater depth in Chapter Eleven.

SUMMARISING THE HORSES' VIEWPOINT

Sensing, Smelling, and Understanding

The questions asked in this chapter give a few answers but, in fact, raise many more questions.

From what the horses themselves revealed, and from Julie's observations over the years, the horse's sense of smell is a vital early warning system. It can tell him almost everything he needs to know about us, his fellow horses, and the environment around him. Certainly, our personal, individual smell has an enormous effect on the way a horse reacts to us.

If horses make an assessment of us through their sense of smell, how do they, who are natural plant eaters, react to those of us who are principally carnivorous? For instance, might a stranger smelling heavily of fried sausage and bacon, especially from stressed or badly slaughtered pigs, be regarded with suspicion? If this were so, would the same stranger, on a day when no animal produce of any kind had been eaten, be welcomed warmly? We don't know. So far, it doesn't appear to have been the subject of any investigation or research.

What the world is like to a horse through its highly sensitive nostrils is a potentially fascinating study in itself. One of the questions the horses were asked was whether they were upset by the smell of blood. The answer was a categorical *no*, from one hundred percent of the group. Yet, they are keenly aware of tobacco, alcohol, and the "wrong" kind of perfume, all of which can make certain horses very uncomfortable.

We know that there are considerable variations in sense of smell between human beings, with some of us having a very keen sense and others who are almost "scent-dumb." How about horses? Are there big variations from horse to horse? Do some have a much more developed sense than others? Is there any correlation between how well developed a horse's sense of smell might be and his own colour? Do chestnuts, who smell quite different from bays, also *perceive* smells differently? And, what effect would it have on their behaviour? If one horse in a group appears to be particularly unpopular, is it because of his odour? If the "cheesy scent" Julie detected on a horse in poor health is unpleasant to us, might it not be even more unattractive and off-putting to a fellow horse?

These are areas that appear worthy of serious investigation. It would be valuable to know how much, and in what kinds of ways, smell influences the horse's behaviour and relationship with the world around him.

Herd animals horses may be, but having a herd mentality does not necessarily mean failing to have a mind, and an individual mind at that. What emerges again and again, not only from the questions they have been asked directly, but also from Julie's wide experience over the years, is that horses are remarkably individual. While common themes hold true, there appear to be many levels of intelligence and understanding amongst the equine race, and also varying levels of compassion. Perhaps not every horse is aware of his name, diet requirements, or how to heal his allergies, but undoubtedly, there are many who are.

They need to be asked the appropriate questions and we must be prepared to listen to their answers.

Horses are capable of showing an enormous amount of sensitivity towards us, in fact, to the point where they can sometimes take on responsibility for our moods and ill humour, or even, perhaps, our ailments.

"I've found," said Julie, "that the horses' advice to us is that if we're having a bad day, it's much better if we don't even attempt to ride them. This is especially true where there's a really close relationship between horse and rider. The horse just gets stressed and miserable and very often thinks the rider is upset because of something the horse has done wrong. There's no doubt about how much they pick up on our moods and, for an extra sensitive horse, it can cause real distress."

If we relay our bad mood to the horse, how does the horse redress his own emotional balance? Not so easily, perhaps, if he's simply put straight back into the stable. The horse has a better chance of unloading our emotional rubbish if he's able to run and roll in the field and work off some of the stress transmitted by his human companions.

Horses, both individually and collectively, appear far more observant and aware of us than we are of them. This must, at times, be a source of real frustration, as some things that are blindingly obvious to them seem to pass us by completely. We may kid ourselves and other people about how we're feeling, but we certainly don't fool a horse.

In the next chapter, we shall take a closer look at how to discover a new level of consciousness between horse and human. Exploring this challenging and exciting area could reveal many unexpected treasures.

CHAPTER II
Four Legs and Talking

How to Communicate with Your Horse

BUT ASK THE ANIMALS AND THEY WILL TEACH YOU, OR THE
BIRDS OF THE AIR, AND THEY WILL TELL YOU: OR SPEAK TO THE
EARTH AND IT WILL TEACH YOU...

Job 12:7,8

A great many people already "ask the animals" but, perhaps, don't always hear their answers. Or sometimes, alas, as in the next story, prefer not to hear them.

One evening Julie received a call from the owner of a show pony who said that he bit her daughter whenever she went to put his rugs on.

"She couldn't decide," said Julie, "whether she wanted me to come out and see the pony or not. 'What happens,' she said to me, 'if the pony says he doesn't like my daughter? Or, what if we're doing something he doesn't like and we're not prepared to change?'

"In the end, I chose not to go. There seemed no point."

Communication with animals at the level that Julie works depends on love, patience, and an honest, heart-felt respect for the animal. This isn't something that can be faked. Horses are not only more observant of us than we are of them, but are frequently a good deal more perceptive, too.

In Chapter Ten, horses gave us some very specific advice about how we could improve our communication with them. *Observe; watch us; be patient; listen*, they said, and two horses suggested that we *look for the pictures* that they send from their minds to ours.

"When it comes to trying to teach or to explain what I do, it suddenly becomes very complicated," said Julie, "although the essence of it is very, very simple. You don't have to communicate on a verbal level with an animal in order to be able to heal. Just to have the intent of sending unconditional love, and the thought of wanting to help is sufficient. As for the other part, conversations with horses if you like, that to me is secondary although it's what fascinates a lot of people. Obviously, through this I can sometimes pick up things that will help the owner reach a better understanding of his or her horse, especially when it concerns a past incident that may have had a big influence on the horse's present behaviour. Or, I might be able to focus on some point that will help the vets in their diagnosis or treatment.

"If you want to improve communication with your horse or with any animal, at whatever level, love is the first and most important factor. I think everyone accepts that. Then, you need time. Plenty of it. Don't rush, be patient. Keep things very simple. Have no expectations. Place no judgements. Be an observer looking in. Just look and see things as they are. Watch."

∞

The horses' first piece of advice to us is to *observe*. This is what Julie does right from the start.

"As soon as I get near the yard, sometimes even before, I'm paying attention. The moment I get out of the car, I'm smelling the air, getting a feel of the general surroundings, sensing what's going on. Is it quiet? Noisy?

Peaceful? Busy? How do I feel when I walk on the yard? Am I comfortable and at ease? Or, do I feel in the way? Although I've been invited, is there some kind of underlying turbulence? Am I walking into negativity? Or is the atmosphere open, welcoming? When I meet the person, do I feel positive, or is a brick wall coming up? Do I feel there's open awareness, a peacefulness? Or, am I picking up frustration or idle curiosity? I'm registering all this silently. It's not judgement or criticism. It's just sensing and observing.

"When I go to meet the horse, I'm conscious of how the person and the horse react to one another. Is the person worried? Are they defensive? Aggressive? Bumptious? Is there a negative feeling between me the person, and the horse? All this sort of observation is going on while we're having normal, everyday chitchat about the weather or the state of the lanes or whatever.

"Of course," Julie continued, "while I'm observing away, so is the horse. He's sussing me out the whole time. He knows I'm coming before I've even arrived. I've hardly got in the yard before he's busy picking up how I look, move, smell—deciding what he thinks about me.

"When I'm asking the owner to give me a general run down on the horse, I'm taking in information about the box. How big is it; is it cold and dark, or bright and airy? Where are the windows, the feeding buckets; how deep is the straw? What does it smell like? How would you feel if you were a horse in there? Would you be comfortable and cosy? Would you feel safe and secure? Or, would it feel like a prison?

"All the time, I'm aware of how the horse is responding to me. Does he mind me being in his space? What's the general feeling as I walked in? Is he wary? Afraid? Does he feel cornered and suspect something unpleasant is going to happen? Is he at ease but in pain somewhere? How does he feel mentally? Confused? Upset? Contented? Sad? Happy? Is he rugged or unrugged? Is he comfortable or uncomfortable with the rugs?"

Julie paused.

"I have to say that if the horse is rugged up, I will never take the rug off. Silly though it sounds, if you undo the straps in a different order or take the rug off in a different way from the owner, it can really cause agitation. It's the kind of thing that can just set up an atmosphere and I want to keep things as pleasant and calm as possible. So I won't ever tack up or put rugs on or off. I always ask the owner to do it."

It also gives a further opportunity for observation.

"I can see how the horse reacts to the owner's handling. Are the ears going back, are the teeth gnashing, does he mind someone going round the rear end? What does the horse feel as the leg straps are coming off? How sensitive is he? Does his stance change? Does the atmosphere change? Does the horse become prickly or stay peaceful? At what point is there agitation, if any, when the rug comes off? Which side? Which leg? Is he happy with the owner doing that? Is the horse standing still or moving around?"

At this point, the owner is usually given pen and pad and invited to make notes as Julie works her way around the horse.

"I like people to sit down in the box, if possible, and be in a passive position, not towering over the horse. That is, of course, as long as it's not dangerous. If they're happy sitting in the stable, looking at the horse at eye level, everything calms down.

"I think, for a lot of owners, it may be the first time they've ever just sat in the stable with the horse. Of course, while all this is going on, the horse is taking in information, too. He's totally aware of how the owner's feeling, how I'm reacting, and what I do if he starts to prance about a bit. Am I calm or stressed? If it looks as if he's going to bite, what do I do? How do I react?"

The second stage in Julie's work follows the horses' advice to be *patient*.

"Underneath all this, I'm silently asking the horse if I have his permission to speak with him. 'Would you like me to help you?' I always ask. If the answer is *yes*, then I proceed. But if it's *no*, and sometimes that happens, then I would ask if I should go away and come back in a minute. Very often then the answer is *yes*. Often, I'm seeing other horses and the uncertain horse wants to wait and see what it's like—get a report back from the others. If the horse says he doesn't want me to go near him, then I ask where he wants me to be, where he considers a safe place for me to stand, and I go and stand there. Then, I stay where I am, remaining calm, and peaceful, and centred.

"Everything has to be done in the horse's own time. I always make the horse come to me and I'll just wait until he does. I keep sending unconditional love, and then, when the horse is ready, he will tell me what he wants me to know—where the pain is, whether he's got a headache or his back hurts or whatever.

"By this point, the horse is coming in to me. I won't have any aggression. I won't have backsides presented to me, either, unless the horse needs reassurance or wants me to scratch his tail."

In the final stages of the session, the horses' request for us to *listen* is honoured and respected.

"Horses make their own decision about everything I do with them. Everything is dominated by what they want. When I'm giving them healing, sometimes they want it for a short time, sometimes much longer. Whether it's thirty seconds or thirty minutes doesn't make it any more profound. The body is like a sponge and it can only soak in so much at a time. I listen to what they want.

"By now, the horse is generally yawning, licking, chewing, the eyes have softened—all the classic signs of relaxation. Sometimes, the horse has things to say for me to relay to his owner, sometimes he doesn't. It all depends on the horse. Everything is his choice. I never intrude, I never push. I'm there to listen and to serve the animal as best I can.

"When the healing is finished and the horse has had enough, then I thank him for the privilege of being able to converse with him and work with him and for allowing me into his private space. Finally, I say thank you to God for using me as a vessel."

∞

Translating what Julie does into our own communication with the horse, or with any animal, can be summed up in three words: watch, wait, and listen.

Here is her advice:

Watch

"If you want to experiment, to test things out for yourself, I'd suggest, first of all, getting to know your horse really well. Just spend some time sitting in the stable with him. Do your knitting, read a book, write a letter. But just be there, quietly observing him. If it's a nice day, go out in the field and see how he gets on with other horses—how they interact with him. Just watch him and be together, quietly, not doing anything in particular. Keep your own mind clear and free. Your watching, your observing, needs to be detached and uncritical.

"Once you start making judgements, then honest observation becomes difficult. Of course, you don't need to tell anyone what you're doing, if you don't want to, especially if you think they're going to ridicule it or be unsympathetic. All this is silent work, between you and the animal."

Wait

"Most people lead such busy lives, they don't allow themselves enough time just to stand and stare. You need to be able to do that with an animal, you need to wait until the horse is ready to accept you and trust you. Not all horses are equally chatty or have a lot to communicate and anyway they don't always want to just when you think they should. The whole process is one of waiting on the animal and respecting his wishes.

"If you push matters too hard or too fast, it will simply make life more difficult for both of you. If you're used to meditating or following a spiritual practice that teaches you to empty your mind and be still, all this will be much easier for you. It's necessary to free your own mind of any junk, so to speak, so that you become a clear canvas for the animal to send you any pictures or messages that he wants you to have.

"In the process of waiting, you need to be open and still, without a lot of distractions. If you've had a busy day or you know you're upset or stressed by something, then don't be too hard on yourself and wait until you're calm. Be aware of how you're feeling so that you're not projecting anything onto the horse.

"I've noticed over the years that a lot of horses mirror their owner's condition, so if the rider has a bad back or a stiff neck, very often, the horse will too. They interact with us at such a deep level. Wait until you're in a calm frame of mind. The same principles apply whether you're seeking a better relationship with a horse, a cat, a dog, or a guinea pig. Be relaxed and receptive.

"From what I see, the biggest difficulty is for people to examine themselves and how they communicate. As humans, we never see it as us being the problem, it's always the horse who's stupid. If we put ourselves in the mind and body of the animal, even for just a little while, we would understand so much more."

Listen

"If you observe and wait, the animal will eventually give you a signal that begins to resonate with you. He may lift a leg, nod his head, or move his ears in a particular way, but from your silent contact, there will eventually be some clear sign that the horse has heard you and is making a reply. It may be in the form of a picture in your mind, nothing that can be seen outwardly. You may get a sudden rush of feeling in your body or such a strong inner knowing that it leaves no room for doubt.

"This is the point, for a lot of people, where they come to a kind of crossroads. They suddenly become unsure whether they've imagined it or whether what they're getting is so off-the-wall that it couldn't possibly be true. When I get messages like the one about the bluebird toffee box, or the horse who wanted a gin and tonic, it's not up to me to censor that out and say it's ridiculous.

"When you start listening to your intuition and hear what the animals are trying to tell you, you have to be in an open and uncritical frame of mind. I'm not saying be gullible and foolish, but just be accurate and honest. It may take a bit of practice and perseverance. It may take a while before you and your animal develop a personal code. If you were telling someone else what your animal said, the language that you use may well be completely different from the way I'd express it. We're all individuals and so is every horse. Communication and healing are like any other skills and no matter how much aptitude you may have, they still improve with the right kind of practice and perseverance.

"For me now, when I receive certain images, I find they're almost always associated with specific conditions or emotions. Over time, you'll find your own. There's no way you can legislate or predict these things. You can't give someone an absolute formula and expect it to work for every individual and every animal one hundred percent of the time.

"There is no right or wrong way, except in the broadest sense of having love in your heart and a high intent. Communication with an animal isn't a trick or a parlour game or a competition. The whole point and purpose of it is to achieve a deeper, happier, more respectful relationship between us and the animals who share our lives.

"It's a process of learning and growing spiritually and respecting the spirit in every living creature. All anyone can do is offer guidelines, ideas, and it's up to each one of us to find our individual way through the maze. From what I see, especially with so-called 'problem' horses, the problem almost always lies with the human being.

"Don't be afraid to trust your own intuition and your own inner guidance. That, and the love you have for your animal, will bring healing to both of you, and allow you to have a friendship that will give you both real joy. Animals are here to teach us about love and to help us heal."

∞

Many people have already instinctively and intuitively adopted this kind of approach and found the benefits enormous. Kate and Bobbie, whose story appeared in Chapter Five, have long since found that they can communicate much more effectively when there is a mutual understanding or code that they have developed. During the two bruising years when Bobbie was recovering from a potentially crippling leg injury, Kate learned a lot.

"I think I'm now much more aware of everything I say and do around the horse. If I'm going to do something, I'll ask Bobbie's opinion before I do it. We seem to have worked out an arrangement. When he touches my hand with his nose, it means *yes*, and for *no*, he just doesn't respond, or he turns his head away. He does it with my partner, too. He knew nothing about horses until he met me, but he respects Bobbie as he'd respect another human being.

"Every six months, I have Bobbie's saddle checked, his teeth checked, and his back given a once over. I do everything in my power to listen to him and try to give him as much choice as possible. I ask him which fetlock boots he wants to wear, whether he wants his rug on or not, if something is too tight or not comfortable. But, I have to say, I don't ask him whether or not he wants to do any work because he'd probably say he'd rather not!"

Recently, Kate began jumping Bobbie again, something that would have been considered absolutely impossible two years earlier. It was not her decision. It was made by the horse himself who, when turned out in the school where several jumps were standing, popped over them on his own initiative.

"When I saddled him up and before I rode him over them, I made sure that they weren't too high. I only jumped him up to two foot six and he seemed fine. Then I put the upright to three foot but, when I put up a spread, he jumped it enthusiastically enough although somehow he just didn't feel right.

"So I decided to ask him what he wanted and what he was comfortable with. I told him that we'd walk around the jumps and if there was one he didn't like, to stop and I'd take that for *no*, and, if he walked on, I'd take it as a *yes*. We rode by the upright, three-foot jump, and I asked him the question and said, 'Stop, if it's too high.' He just ambled on, ears going back and forth. When we rode by the spread, I asked him if it was too wide. He stopped, and I could see that he considered it was."

The degree of sensitivity and attention that Kate has put into communication with Bobbie is enormous and it has brought rewards to both horse and rider.

"A lot of people say they want to communicate with animals, but when it comes down to it, they're not prepared to make the effort. Animals have their own mind, their own thoughts, and to have a good relationship with them, you have to work at it. If we understand them better, we can give them greater freedom of choice. Do they want to be rugged up? What kind of boots do they prefer? Would they rather be in the stable or in the field?

"Freedom of choice is good for them. It's good for us too, because it removes the burden of anxiety. You know they're having what they really want and you're making them happy."

∞

Healing and communication are about raising the quality of life for animals, and ultimately, for us as well.

Working with the suggestions that Julie has made will bring us into a new kind of relationship with our animals. But, unlike the owner at the start of this chapter, we have to be willing to change, to open our minds to new possibilities, to new attitudes, and new ways of working with animals.

Change, for most of us, is sometimes challenging, sometimes exciting, and sometimes daunting, or even frightening. If we change our attitude towards the animal kingdom, what will happen to them and to us? What will life be like if we succeed in "talking with the animals"?

Some things will alter almost at once. We shall never again to be able to repeat or pay lip service to that old cliché, known to every owner and probably everyone who's ever come within patting distance of a horse, "Now then, don't forget—you've got to make him respect you!"

Of course, boundaries have to be made and human safety respected. But, this advice will no longer be offered as the golden rule when establishing good relations with a horse, or indeed any animal. In fact, the first rule is not *he* must respect *us*, but *we* must understand *him*! Putting the animal first may be a new concept for some, but it is one that will ultimately pay enormous dividends.

Arabian breeder Malcolm remarked, "I think we all find great solace in animals and maybe it's through them that many of us can find our way to God. Animals can give us spiritual enlightenment, and if we respect them as they deserve to be respected, they can help us become better human beings."

Communication at the deeper level that we have presented in this book, at the level beyond the five senses, important though they are, can only bring benefits to animals and humans alike. We will become more receptive, more aware, more respectful, and much kinder to all living creatures, whether they possess two legs or four. We will come to know animals as real friends and fellow travellers on the planet, rather than creatures who we must dominate or manipulate for our own ends. They, in turn, will flourish and give us love and healing.

The joy of this more creative approach allows us all to be pioneers in a new frontier of consciousness, if we so choose. We don't need to be a particular age, sex, colour, or creed. We need no special education, apart from an openness of heart and mind. We don't need to wait for our family, friends and neighbours or theologians, politicians or scientists, to give us their authority or their blessing. All we need is love, patience, observation, and willingness to do whatever we can to improve the lives of the animals for whom we act as guardians.

Communicating with animals at the deepest level is silent work, but we are all capable of hearing the silence and seeing the invisible. Through what we have felt and experienced for ourselves will come an inner peace, reflected in our own lives and those of our animals. If we ask them, and if we listen, the animals will teach us. We will find that what we know to be true in the silence of the mind and the heart, no one can ever take away.

CHAPTER 12

Pioneers in Consciousness

Observations and Ethics

T he stories in this book are true and factual. Out of respect for
their privacy, only the names of the individuals have been
altered.

However, the quotation above neatly sums up some of the difficulty
in trying to decipher the mysteries of animal consciousness and the ways
that human beings can communicate directly with the heart and mind of
the animal. There are endless snags, pitfalls, and traps, and weaving a route
amongst them is fraught with hazard, especially for anyone who is looking
for objective proof that these tales are indeed true.

Can a horse really decide on the owner it wants, and figure out that
the best way to do it is by going lame? Is a horse capable of knowing which
shoes suit it best? Or, what medicine it needs? Are horses able to show real
compassion for one another as well as for us? If so, then horses are indeed

capable of reason and of emotions similar to our own. We are now in the realm of anthropomorphism—the attributing of human thoughts and emotions to animals.

All the stories you've read are anecdotal evidence of what horses think and feel, relayed through one individual's perceptions and understanding. However, because this is subjective evidence and not objective, it is not scientifically sound. If it is not scientifically sound, that is can be proved through objective means, can it be true? How would you set about proving that we can honestly attribute to horses the ideas and feelings that have been put forth in this book? What scientific trials and surveys could you use?

It is this very problem of trying to find a model upon which to base research that bedevils the whole question of animal consciousness, which, in turn, impacts the highly emotive area of animal welfare. Dr. Marian Stamp Dawkins of Oxford University, a scientist of considerable authority in the field of animal consciousness writes, "It is hard to think of any other subject that touches so deeply on so many important issues. Unfortunately, it is also hard to think of anything else that is quite so difficult and intractable to study either."

How much proof we need, though, is a question that not all scientists are agreed upon. Psychologist Masson and biologist McCarthy, in their book, *When Elephants Weep,* state, "The standards for defining the existence of emotions in animals should be the same as those in common use for humans. One should no more demand proof that an animal feels an emotion than would be demanded of a human—and like humans, the animal should be permitted to speak its own emotional language, which it is up to the beholder to understand."

It is the "speaking of its own emotional language" that we have been dealing with in this book, and our interpreter has been Julie Dicker. How can we verify what she has found to be true in an objective manner when the very nature of what she does is beyond the realm of the five physical senses?

Professor Donald Griffin, formerly of Harvard University, one of the most respected pioneers in this difficult arena considers that, "...scientists commonly err by being too sceptical and refusing to accept evidence at its face value when it challenges established beliefs. Field observers often fail to report evidence suggestive of conscious thinking even when they obtain it, and editors of scientific journals are reluctant to publish it."

Although from the scientist's viewpoint, finding an objective and rigorous method of assessing consciousness continues to be a challenge, for most animal owners anthropomorphism is not a heretical belief.

Masson and McCarthy ask, "Why do most people consider it obvious that animals they are close to have emotions, while most scientists consider it not only far from obvious but positively wrong, pernicious, and unscientific?"

Jane Goodall, renowned for her work with chimpanzees, says, "If we are prepared to admit that we are not the only beings with personality, that we are not the only beings capable of rational thought, and above all, not the only beings capable of emotions similar to—sometimes even identical to—those that we call happiness, sadness, fear, despair, and suffering, then that leads to a new respect, not just for chimpanzees but through them for all the animal kingdom."

In a recent behavioural study of sheep at the Babraham Institute at Cambridge, Dr Keith Kendrick has established that sheep can recognise up to fifty individuals, human or sheep. He comments, "...if they have the same kind of ability as ourselves in one of the most difficult mental activities we do, their intelligence and their relationships may be much greater and more complex than we thought."

The attribution of emotions and reason to horses, so closely and intimately connected with mankind for many thousands of years, should not be so astonishing. In fact, it's worth taking a closer look at how all of us, not just the scientific community, actually are attributing human thoughts to animals the whole time.

There's often a good deal of inconsistency in our approach, which tends to be more obviously apparent in the horse world, where we indulge in what might be called "positive" or "negative" anthropomorphism, depending on our state of mind.

When a human being is having trouble with a horse, something most horse owners will agree occurs from time to time, there are a number of clichés that are commonly trotted out. "You've got to show him who's boss." "You mustn't let him get away with it." "He's just playing you up." "You've got to teach that horse a lesson." And, of course, the much favoured phrase that acts as the summation of these principles: "They've got to respect you!" All these well-worn remarks actually indicate that we're ascribing human emotions and thoughts to an animal. In other words, we are guilty of anthropomorphism. Negative anthropomorphism, that is. We're attributing the horse with undesirable human characteristics.

"You've got to show him who's boss." This suggests, given half a chance, the horse will run the show and take over our role as leader. Indeed, he might, if we prove to be ineffective at the task. It also implies that "he" has a mind; that "he" is capable of making choices and is equally capable of asserting which choice he wants to make.

If this is so, why should we automatically assume his choice is less valid than ours? Nobody would deny that horses require and appreciate strong, clear leadership but that doesn't mean domination.

"You mustn't let him get away with it." Often used when the horse has done something of which we don't approve. It can be as innocuous as refusing to have a bit in the mouth when it has a searing toothache; mistakenly supposing the carrot you offered included your fingers; or showing absolute terror when asked to walk through, what seems to us, a perfectly innocent puddle of water.

We are sometimes encouraged, if we are to behave like a "proper" leader, to inflict some form of punishment on the horse in order to "teach him a lesson." But, of course, the deed that we're so keen to correct, the act that "he mustn't get away with," is more often than not caused by fear, pain, or failure to understand what we want him to do. But the implication of "not letting him get away with it" is that the horse has given thought to its actions and is now deliberately trying to thwart us in every possible way it can.

"He's just playing you up" is another favourite, often used when a horse has successfully performed some operation umpteen times in a row and then declares it has had enough by saying so in the only way it can. Unfortunately, this declaration of independence can take the form of depositing the rider on the ground or simply standing stock still and refusing to budge in any direction.

However, "He's just playing you up," is another indication that we consider this to be a deliberate, thought out action on the part of the horse; thereby implying not only does he have a mind capable of reason but is also manipulative, rather than simply responding to discomfort, boredom, or plain misunderstanding as a result of the often confusing signals we're sending him.

Followers of the "You've got to show him who's boss" school often advocate some form of punishment for many kinds of so-called equine misbehaviour, since it is believed this will then bring about the ultimate aim, namely that the horse will "respect you."

We're sanguine enough about attributing negative traits to the horse, like stubbornness, aggression, laziness, stupidity, a tendency to manipulate, all characteristics, alas, well known in the human race. In short, we are comfortable with *negative* anthropomorphism.

However, when we ascribe to horses and other animals the higher emotions we generally consider to be our sole property: love, loyalty, generosity of spirit, courage, loneliness, and grief, we are a lot less comfortable. This is the realm of *positive* anthropomorphism and many of us get extremely uneasy when we enter it. Indeed, it can make all kinds of things very difficult for us in our relationship with animals.

If animals feel loneliness the way we do, should we leave them without companions of their own kind for hours on end? If they suffer from grief, how much more sensitive do we need to be when we take away their young? Or, if they forge close friendships, do we sell that friend without so much as a thought for the one left behind? Our treatment of all animals, from the farm to the laboratory, becomes increasingly disturbing if they have a greater awareness than we're willing to credit them.

In medicine, huge ethical questions are constantly raised that involve an ever-widening range of animals. Is it appropriate to keep pregnant mares tethered in stalls, twenty-four hours a day, their bladders permanently drained for six months of the year, so that their urine may be harvested for use in hormone-replacement therapy? In the field of xenotransplantation— the transference of animal organs to humans—does the pig, whose liver is being donated to a human being, suffer as much as the human, or possibly more so? If he does, do we have any right to demand that the animal be sacrificed for us?

What of laboratory animals? Rats, mice, and guinea pigs have long played a role in the development of new frontiers in medicine. What about the use of primates, some of whom are even able to use sign language to communicate with us? Should we continue to make any experiments at all involving animals? Is the argument that their suffering lessens the suffering of mankind a credible one?

How about fish? Recent research has shown that they're able to recognise certain bars of music. Does this indicate a level of consciousness that they're not normally believed to possess? If so, should we treat them differently? In what way? Should we hunt or kill any wild animals at all, for any purpose whatever? Even for food? Do we have the right to alter our domestic animals by declawing cats or docking dogs tails?

Many individuals have been asking questions like these for years. They're not new. But now, stimulated by the enormous and far-reaching effects of biotechnology and the cloning and genetic modification of animals, there are more questions than ever before. They are so daunting and so harrowing that for most of us, it is an easier option to close our eyes and ears and take the line of least resistance. Science and ethics are now bedfellows and science appears to be posing questions faster than ethics can answer.

If it's hard for us, as animal owners, to be scrupulously fair in our attitude towards them, then it can be even harder for the scientist to disengage from his feelings and enter the mental laboratory where the animal's emotions are dissected as sharply as the scalpel that cuts the flesh. When faced with this contentious issue, many scientists display the wariness of a horse viewing a plastic bag in the hedgerow and behave in much the same manner. They have a tendency to turn and run.

As Masson and McCarthy point out, "...emotion is regarded as so dangerous an area that it should not be part of the scientific agenda—such a minefield of subjectivity that no investigation of it should take place. As a result, none but the most prominent scientists risk their reputations and credibility by venturing into this area."

For scientists seeking to examine animal feelings in objective terms, the vocabulary used to describe human emotions is not considered acceptable when it is applied to animals, since it cannot easily be verified by the current research models. This certainly poses immense difficulties in trying to find a scientific model that will allow the problem of animals' minds and emotions to be satisfactorily researched. Furthermore, since most published scientific work relies upon the work of other scientists to verify it, we come to a situation that can only be called a catch-22.

However, the fact that something is difficult to pin down in a scientific manner using rules that science itself has formulated to test the soundness of a hypothesis should not negate the very existence of the hypothesis.

If scientists have not yet found a satisfactory methodology for testing their views on the matter of animal mind and emotion, there's nothing to stop the rest of us exercising a more balanced form of anthropomorphism. This includes acknowledging that if we're prepared to consider that a horse can deliberately "play you up" then it's only fair to acknowledge, equally, that it could also show compassion and concern towards you, as did the pony who was worried over a child's grazed knee.

A balanced form of anthropomorphism means we're seeing the animal holistically, giving equal respect to its mental and emotional needs just as much as recognising its physical requirements. There's no reason why this kind of approach should encourage a false or misplaced sentimentality; quite the reverse in fact, because it takes into account *all* the animal's needs and requirements as an *animal* and not as a surrogate human being. Just as importantly, it recognises that animals have a mind and an emotional life and that we are willing to respect and honour all aspects of their being.

If it is difficult to find a scientific model for testing animal consciousness, it's equally difficult to find one for verifying the concept of mind-to-mind communication. It's easy to see why the whole area of non-physical communication between humans and animals is, from the scientific point of view, almost impossible. How do you measure it? How do you even regard something that is so ephemeral?

The physicist David Bohm introduced the idea of the "implicate order" or another kind of reality where everything is enfolded into everything and all information is stored. Perhaps, in the vast sea of energy that some quantum physicists now call the "Zero Point Field" lie the answers to what might appear a mysterious connection between the mind of animal and human. The condition of "oneness," where there is no separation either from God or any living being, is a deeply familiar theme in almost every mystic's journey. Yet, it is this oneness that links the mystic to the scientist in the area of non-physical communication.

Gary Zukav writes that the "...philosophical implication of quantum mechanics is that all of the things in our universe (including us) that appear to exist independently are actually parts of one all-encompassing organic pattern and that no parts of that pattern are ever really separate from it or from each other."

However, in order to access this information from the "all-encompassing organic pattern" or energetic sea, it seems likely that we need to be in a particular state of consciousness, where our brain pattern is able to pick up and receive the waves sent out from this central field. Certainly, anyone in a high state of irritation emerging from a three-hour trawl around a major city at rush hour is not going to be emitting the kind of waves that permit either healing or a meditative frame of mind.

Lynne McTaggert, writing of the work of Dr. William Braud in ESP, or extra-sensory perception, says, "When two people 'relax' their bandwidths and attempt to establish some kind of deep connection, their brain patterns become highly synchronised." It appears that the most ordered brain pattern always prevails and she goes on to say, "In this circumstance, a type of 'coherent domain' gets established..."

Dr. Caroline Myss, a theologian, medical intuitive, and considerable authority in this field talks of "Mastering the science of interpreting energetic information," which is indeed what every sensitive involved in working with the non-physical world must learn to do. Alas, the way in which information is transmitted energetically is not always easy to translate, as we saw in the "Bluebird" story, or, indeed, with Cedric and his shoes, where a personal system of question and answer, through pictures, revealed what the horse wanted. His request turned out to be perfectly viable, as the amused farrier subsequently verified.

Information can also be received through the "inner voice," which is not necessarily a voice but often a concept, which we loosely define as a "voice." Information may also be transmitted via an image or picture.

Although the energy containing the information might, in itself, be quite impersonal or objective and could be picked up by ten different sensitives, it still has to be interpreted in a context that's compatible with the individual sensitive's frame of reference, which includes their cultural and educational background.

In other words, the energy wave or band through which the information or the concept is travelling, is itself, *impersonal*. But, the way it is interpreted by an individual is highly *personal* and therefore 'subjective.' Since objectivity is essential to scientific investigation, this proves a serious problem for conventional research. Apart from the information, which may or may not immediately resonate with the sensitive's own understanding, it must also be put in a way, as Julie points out, "that people can take on board and accept."

During the late sixties and early seventies, a remarkable spiritual textbook, *A Course in Miracles,* was "channelled" by Dr. Helen Schucman. It has been described as a "self study course designed to shift our perceptions, heal our minds and change our behaviour."

In the early stages of the work, which took a period of seven years, Dr. Schucman was often tempted to change parts of the script that did not make sense to her own academic training. But, inevitably, as the work progressed and the teaching became clearer to her, she realised that what she had first "heard," or intuited, had been correct and she was obliged to return to the original text.

As a highly trained research psychologist, she was deeply wary and mistrustful of anything that might even remotely resemble the psychotic state, where some unfortunate soul hears "voices," often urging him to commit strange or undesirable acts. There was nothing hallucinatory about Dr. Schucman's experiences, however, and the "voice" did not come from outside. "It's all internal," she wrote. "There's no sound and the words come mentally but very clearly. It's a kind of inner dictation, you might say."

However, no matter how much sensitives might have in common, and there are far more similarities than differences, each one still remains highly individual, and the style in which energetic information is relayed has many variations.

When, in 1995, the first of a number of channelled books by Neil Donald Walsch, *Conversations with God,* was published, it used American idioms in a way that reflected his earlier career in US radio and journalism. In contrast, the literary style of *A Course in Miracles* is more academic than popular, more restrained than colloquial. Although both works emanate from a spiritual source and contain much of the same philosophy, and although both "interpreters" or "channels" are from the same side of the Atlantic, the literary style in which their inspiration is transcribed is markedly different.

Since information coming from a non-physical source inevitably appears to be couched in the language and phraseology of the individual who is transcribing it, sometimes the language leads to confusion or misunderstanding. This can cause considerable doubt about its authenticity, especially to the well-trained academic or scientific mind; so much so that the essence of the message itself is often either lost or negated. This is perhaps even more evident in the field of mind-to-mind communication with animals, where there is still less margin for checking the validity of the information than is the case with human beings.

Dr. Nic Rowley, subtitling one of his books on clinical science, *Describing a Rose with a Ruler,* gives a helpful analogy for this apparent confusion over the relaying of energetic material. He likens the differences in interpretation to someone looking at a picture with a caption in a language foreign to our own. Each person will define or translate the caption slightly differently, as they put it into their native tongue. And, some will not define the words at all, but simply describe the picture.

After all, if any of us were to ask six friends to tell us about a movie they'd all seen or write a report on a book they'd all read, there would be a common thread of ideas and themes. But, no two accounts would be identical; nor would we expect them to be.

In order to maintain their integrity, individual sensitives have to find a way to carry out an internal audit that enables them to have a sense of certainty about the information they've received and are being asked to relay. They have to reach the point where, as Julie said, "It isn't as if you *think* it's right. You *know* it is."

This is not a dogmatic statement, dictated by arrogance and egocentricity. Rather, it is the reverse. It's a statement of inner confidence and trust, coupled with humility. The intuitive individual is effectively saying, "Look, I don't believe this information is coming from my conscious mind because it is out of my framework of knowledge and understanding. But, here it is. Make of it what you will!"

It takes courage to do this because it is pitifully easy for the logical mind to destroy the wisdom of the heart. Our linear, rational, logical left brain, dealing comfortably with words and numbers, is at home in the world of our physical senses. But, our intuitive right brain, seeing patterns, pictures, possibilities rather than words and numbers, permits us to make leaps of imagination. The left brain then does it's best to translate this into something definable, which conforms to its own sense of logic. Very often, logic wins over intuition, and the warfare that exists between the two halves, archetypically demonstrated by the old clichés, "Feminine intuition" and "Masculine logic" is still very real.

Gary Zukav writes, "Our entire society reflects a left hemispheric bias (it is rational, masculine and assertive). It gives very little reinforcement to those characteristics representative of the right hemisphere (intuitive, feminine, receptive)."

Here, in a nutshell, lies the dilemma that confronts many ordinary individuals when they get involved in a world they don't think they can see, taste, touch, smell, or hear. The operative word here is *think*. The mind can only make some of the connections; the heart has to feel the rest and bring them back for the mind to grapple with: facts versus possibilities; sensory data versus intuitive data; male versus female; science versus religion.

The list of opposing areas is endless, each area valid and each one prompted by the different halves that form the very physiology of our brains. Yet, what is beyond the brain, beyond the mental confines, is what we're dealing with in our efforts to understand the animal kingdom from the perspective of non-physical communication.

To have any degree of success here, the integration of both sides, heart and mind, is essential. Getting to the stage where there is honest clarity, where a distinction can be made between energetic material from a higher source and material that is not, is a process of discernment that every sensitive has to undergo for himself. It's not an easy task, and it demands a high level of discipline and the constant practice of honest self-appraisal. Equally important, everyone listening to, or reading material from, what purports to be another level of consciousness, has to make his or her own assessment as to its integrity and worth. The basic tenet of the Hippocratic oath, that you should do no harm, applies equally strongly to both the giving and receiving of energetic information or what some sources call "remote viewing."

It looks more and more as though it is essential for us to evolve, as Zukav says, "from five sensory humans into multi-sensory humans." He points out that our five senses—sight, sound, smell, taste, and touch—are designed to perceive physical reality but, "The perceptions of a multi-sensory human extend beyond physical reality…The multi-sensory human is able to perceive and to appreciate the role that our physical reality plays in a larger picture of evolution and the dynamics by which our physical reality is created and sustained. This realm is invisible to the five-sensory human."

Our world is shifting very fast. New scientific models are being created and new discoveries made on an almost daily basis, especially in the field of quantum physics. Science writer and journalist Lynne McTaggert pulls together many of the recent and remarkable findings by physicists around the globe in her book, *The Field*. She writes that, "The coming scientific revolution heralded the end of dualism in every sense. Far from destroying God, science for the first time was proving His existence—by demonstrating that a higher, collective consciousness was out there. There need no longer be two truths, the truth of science and the truth of religion. There could be one unified version of the world."

Such a vision would, at last, allow animals to be liberated from the prison that our logical mind has made for them and enable them to share their wisdom with us.

In *Kinship with All Life,* J. Allen Boone wrote of the importance of being an animal educator and allowing only the highest and best thoughts to pass between you and the animal. "Moving into the situation with insight and intuition, he places full emphasis on the mental rather than on the physical part of the animal. He treats it as an intelligent fellow being whose capacity for development and expression he refuses to limit in any direction. He seeks to help the animal make use of its thinking faculties..."

To see animals, not as mechanistic creatures, nor as ones to be exploited or manipulated at will by us, but as whole beings, of mind, body, and spirit would be an amazing step forward, not just for the animal kingdom, but for the human race.

In 1985, Professor Tom Regan said, "All great movements, it is written, go through three stages: ridicule, discussion, adoption. It is the realisation of this third stage, adoption, that requires both our passion and our discipline, our hearts and our heads. The fate of animals is in our hands. God grant that we are equal to the task."

God grant it indeed.

REFERENCES AND SELECTED BIBLIOGRAPHY

Ainslie, Tom & Ledbetter, Bonnie, *The Body Language of Horses,* William Morrow & Co., New York, USA, 1980.

Blake, Henry, *Talking with Horses,* Souvenir Press, UK, and Trafalgar Square, USA, 1997.

Blake, Henry, *Thinking with Horses,* Souvenir Press, UK, and Trafalgar Square, USA, 1993.

Bohm, David, *Wholeness and the Implicate Order,* Routledge, 2000, USA/UK.

Boone, J. Allen, *Kinship with All Life,* Harper & Row, UK, and Harper San Francisco, USA, 1976.

Boone, J. Allen. *The Language of Silence: Communication between Human Beings and Animals,* Harper & Row, 1970, USA/UK.

Boy Who Saw True, The, C W Daniel and Company, UK, 1998.

Course in Miracles, A, Foundation for Inner Peace, California, USA, 1975.

Darwin, Charles, *The Expression of the Emotions in Man and Animals,* Harper Collins, New York, USA, 1999.

Dawkins, Marion Stamp, *Through Our Eyes Only?* Oxford University Press, UK, 1998.

Dossey, Larry, *Recovering the Soul: A Scientific and Spiritual Search,* Bantam Books, 1989, USA/UK.

Dossey, Larry, *Space, Time & Medicine,* Shambhala Publications, Massachussetts, USA, 1982.

Evans, George Ewart, *The Horse in the Furrow,* Faber & Faber, London, UK, 1960.

Fitzpatrick, Sonya, *Cat Talk: The Secrets of Communicating with Your Cat,* Sidgwick & Jackson, London, UK, and Berkley Publishing Group, New York, USA, 2002.

Fraser, Andrew F., *The Behaviour of the Horse,* Cab International, UK, 1997.

Gawani Pony Boy, *Horse, Follow Closely,* Bowtie Press, California, USA, 1999.

George, Chief Dan, *My Heart Soars,* Hancock House Publishers, Washington, USA, 2000.

Gerber, Richard, *Vibrational Medicine,* Bear and Company, Vermont, USA, 1988.

Goodall, Jane, "Four Reasons for Hope," *Living Lightly,* Issue 13, Autumn 2000.

Griffin, Donald R., *Animal Thinking,* Harvard University Press, Massachussetts, USA, 1994.

Kendrick, Dr. Keith, *Farm and Food Society Journal,* March 2002, 101.

Kiley-Worthington, Marthe, *The Behaviour of Horses,* J.A. Allen, London, UK, 1987, and Breakthrough Publications, Pennsylvania, USA, 1997.

Kiley-Worthington, Marthe, "The Importance of Odour in Human-animal Interaction," *Occasional Paper No. 025*, 1998.

Kinkade, Amelia, *Straight from the Horse's Mouth,* Harper Collins, 2001, USA/UK.

Mackay, Nicci, *Spoken in Whispers,* Mainstream Publishing, UK, 1997, and Fireside, New York, USA, 1998.

Manning, Aubrey, and Stamp Dawkins, Marion, *An Introduction to Animal Behaviour,* Cambridge University Press, UK, 1998.

Masson, Jeffrey, and McCarthy, Susan, *When Elephants Weep,* Vintage, London, UK, 1996.

McCormick, Adele, and Marlena Deborah, *Horse Sense and the Human Heart,* Health Communications Inc, Florida, USA, 1997.

McElroy, Susan Chernak, *Animals as Teachers and Healers,* Ballantine Books, 1997, USA/UK.

McGreevy, Paul, *Why Does My Horse...?* Souvenir Press, UK, 2000.

McTaggart, Lynne, *The Field,* Harper Collins, 2001, USA/UK.

Myss, Caroline, *Anatomy of the Spirit,* Bantam, New York, USA, 1996.

Rashid, Mark, *A Good Horse is Never a Bad Color,* Johnson Books, Colorado, USA, 1996.

Rees, Lucy, *The Horse's Mind,* Stanley Paul, UK, 1984, Arco Publishing, New York, USA, 1985.

Rowley, Nic, *Basic Clinical Science: Describing a Rose with a Ruler,* Hodder & Stoughton, 1994, USA/UK.

Sheldrake, Rupert, *Dogs That Know When Their Owners Are Coming Home: And Other Unexplained Powers of Animals,* Hutchinson, UK, and Three Rivers Press, New York, USA, 2000.

Shine, Betty, *A Free Spirit: Gives You the Right to Make Choices*, Harper Collins, UK, 2001.

Singer, Peter, ed. *In Defence of Animals,* quote by Tom Regan, Blackwell, 1985, USA/UK.

Skipper, Lesley, *Inside Your Horse's Mind,* J.A. Allen, London, UK, 1999.

Swift, Sally, *Centred Riding,* Ebury Press, UK, and Trafalgar Square, Vermont, USA, 1985.

Walsh, Neil Donald, *Conversations with God: An Uncommon Dialogue, Book 3,* Hodder & Stoughton, UK, and Hampton Roads Publishing Co., Virginia, USA, 1998.

Wanless, Mary, *For the Good of the Horse,* Kenilworth Press, UK, and Trafalgar Square, Vermont, USA, 1997.

Wise, Steven M. *Rattling the Cage: Toward Legal Rights for Animals,* Profile Books, London, UK, 2000, and Perseus Publishing, New York, USA, 2001.

Xenophon, *The Art of Horsemanship,* J.A. Allen, London, UK, 1999.

Zukav, Gary, *The Seat of the Soul,* Rider, UK, and Fireside, New York, USA, 1990.

Zukav, Gary, *The Dancing Wu Li Masters: An Overview of the New Physics,* Harper Collins, 2000, USA/UK.

INDEX